everything **twentys**

david edwards ▪ margaret feinberg ▪ janella griggs ▪ matthew paul turner

tyndale house publishers, inc.
carol stream, illinois

Visit Tyndale's exciting Web site at **www.tyndale.com**

TYNDALE is a registered trademark of Tyndale House Publishers, Inc.

Tyndale's quill logo is a registered trademark of Tyndale House Publishers, Inc.

Everything Twentys

PHOTOGRAPHS:
© 2005 by JOHN BAMBER: Pages 2-5, 8, 12, 16-18, 22, 26-27, 33-35, 37, 40, 42-43, 46-49, 54-55, 58-59, 66-67, 70-71, 78-79, 82, 84, 88-89, 92-95, 104-106,108, 114-118, 123, 128-129, 132-133, 139-140, 143, 147, and chapter openers

© 2005 by ERIN HERNER: Pages 9, 17, 19-21, 24, 38, 44, 52, 56-57, 60-63, 92, 100, 121-122, 124-125, 133, 142, and 145

© 2005 by JESS FLEGEL: Pages 4-5, 8, 18-19, 21, 25, 30, 36, 39, 70-71, 77, 81, 86-87, 89-90, 95-96, 98, 100, 106, 110, 120-122, 130, 135-138, 141, and 144-145

© 2005 BY JON MCGRATH: Pages 10-11, 31, 45, and 61

© 2005 BY AMBER BURGER: Pages 16 and 62-63

All rights reserved.

Photographs: Page 111 by Photos.com; Pages 12,17, 60, 69, 76, 83, 109, 120, 141, and 146 Ablestock. All rights reserved.

Illustrations: Pages 64-65 by Luke Daab; Pages 14 and 15 by Jessie McGrath. Copyright 2005 by Tyndale House Publishers.

Designed by JESSIE MCGRATH

Edited by ANNE GOLDSMITH

Worldview Comparison Chart on page 80 used with permission from *Christianity: The Faith That Makes Sense*, by Dennis McCallum, Tyndale House Publishers, 1992.

Unless otherwise indicated, all Scripture quotations are taken from the *Holy Bible*, New Living Translation, copyright © 1996, 2004. Used by permission of Tyndale House Publishers, Inc., Carol Stream, Illinois 60188. All rights reserved.

Scripture quotations marked NASB are taken from the *New American Standard Bible*, © 1960, 1962, 1963, 1968, 1971, 1972, 1973, 1975, 1977 by The Lockman Foundation. Used by permission.

Scripture quotations marked KJV are taken from the *Holy Bible*, King James Version.

Scripture quotations marked NIV are taken from the *Holy Bible*, New International Version ®. NIV ®. Copyright © 1973, 1978, 1984 by International Bible Society. Used by permission of Zondervan. All rights reserved.

Scripture quotations marked *The Message* are taken from *The Message*. Copyright © 1993, 1994, 1995, 1996 by Eugene H. Peterson. Used by permission of NavPress Publishing Group. All rights reserved.

Library of Congress Cataloging-in-Publication Data

Everything twentys / David Edwards ... [et al.].

    p. cm. -- (Twentys)

ISBN-13: 978-1-4143-0555-4 (sc)

ISBN-10: 1-4143-0555-9 (sc)

1. Young adults--Religious life. 2. Christian life. I. Title: Everything twenties. II. Edwards, David, date. III. Series.

BV4529.2E84 2005

248.8'4--dc22

        2005009885

Printed in the United States of America

11 10 09 08 07 06

7 6 5 4 3 2 1

contents

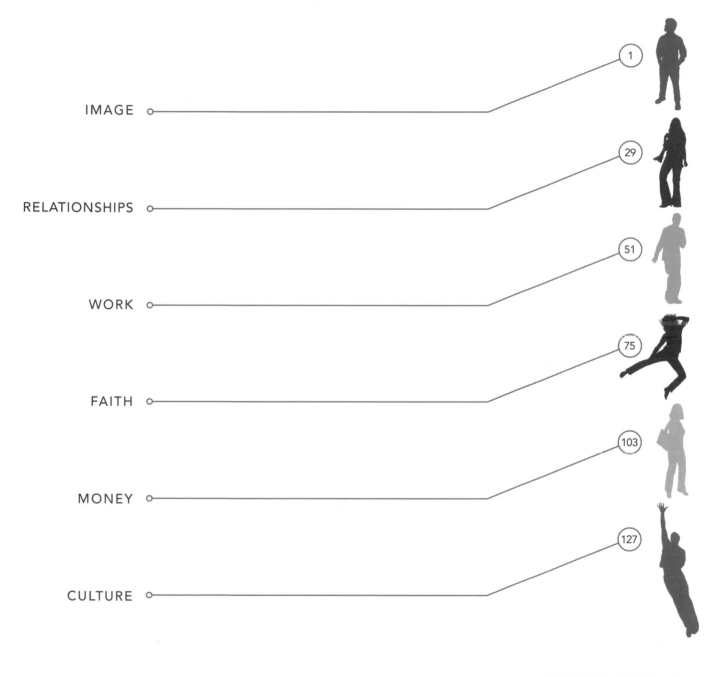

foreword

In 2003 I felt God pulling at my heart to start an organization to mobilize the most powerful people in the world: twentys. With most of their education behind them and almost all of their adult life before, I knew if they could be inspired to make a difference in the world, the world would never be the same. I am more convinced today than ever that my assumptions about twentys are true.

The difficult and stressful decade between 20 and 29 is one of almost constant transition. You transition out of being a teen into an instant chronological adult. You transition from a young adult looking for a job to a more mature adult looking to make a difference. Then you begin to make the transition into your thirties where expectations are higher and life is even more complicated.

When I went through the twentys decade I did not do too well. I botched many relationships and wandered from my convictions. I was anything but authentic as I faked my way through those trying years. I needed help, but no one was volunteering to give it to me. I was a miserable example of how not to live life.

So now I am volunteering to help you have what I did not: great information and inspiration to live the best life and the most meaningful life full of purpose and happiness. This book is part of that effort along with an association, a web community, and events. This is just one way all of us are trying to provide the right stuff so you can do the next right thing. That is what this book is designed to help you do by addressing every area of your life and helping you connect with others in the same search.

The authors have included a very broad list of topics, arranged into different "life components," in an attempt to be as inclusive as possible about everything in your life as a twenty. I know it's called *Everything Twentys*, but I'm sure if you look hard, you will find something missing. They've done a good job, though, in at least highlighting the major highs and lows of life between 20 and 29.

You'll find everything from hilarious spoofs and sarcastic wit to deep spiritual exploration and painful emotional battles. These pages are loaded with great tips and information that is practical and even usable every day for the rest of your life. And all that from a group of very real, honest, and funny people you can trust.

It is my prayer that this book, and everything Twentys as an organization does in the future will help you live a full, balanced and meaningful life as you work to change this world for the better. I have long believed you are the generation to do it, and I can't wait to do all I can to help energize, mobilize, and encourage you to get out there and make the difference. First by having your own life in order and in tune with God's best, and then by reaching out and helping others do the same.

If that is of interest to you, dig into these great words by some of the wisest, funniest, deepest, and, at times, picky-est people I know!

Steve Arterburn
FOUNDER OF TWENTYS

IMAGE—AN INTRODUCTION

MEET SOMEONE NEW IN COLLEGE, AND YOU'RE SURE TO ASK OR BE ASKED THE SAME THREE BORING QUESTIONS: (1) "WHAT'S YOUR NAME?"; (2) "WHERE ARE YOU FROM?"; AND (3) "WHAT'S YOUR MAJOR?" UNFORTUNATELY, THE CREATIVITY OF POLITE CONVERSATION DOESN'T IMPROVE WHEN YOU'RE OUT OF SCHOOL. THE QUESTIONS CHANGE, BUT ONLY SLIGHTLY: (1) "WHAT'S YOUR NAME?"; (2) "WHERE DO YOU LIVE?"; AND (3) "WHAT DO YOU DO?" ISN'T IT DISTURBING THAT YOUR ENTIRE EXISTENCE AS A HUMAN BEING MIGHT BE MEASURED BY THREE SUCH INSIGNIFICANT DETAILS? AS IF WHERE YOU'RE FROM AND WHAT YOU DO COULD POSSIBLY PAINT A CLEAR PICTURE OF THE REAL YOU! OR WHAT ABOUT THOSE CHEESY ALLITERATION GAMES YOU PLAY IN SMALL GROUPS? "I'M FUNNY FRANKLIN," OR "I'M JOLLY JULIE." THOSE ARE EVEN WORSE! ONE WORD SETS THE STAGE FOR HOW THE GROUP WILL REMEMBER YOU FOR THE REST OF YOUR LIFE. BETTER MAKE IT A GOOD ONE. OH, THE PRESSURE! OF COURSE, THOSE GAMES ARE MEANT TO BE SILLY. AND THE BORING QUESTIONS PEOPLE ASK WHEN THEY FIRST MEET YOU ARE REALLY JUST MEANT TO OPEN DOORS TO MORE CONVERSATION. BUT THAT DOES BEG THE QUESTION, WHAT WOULD YOU SAY IF SOMEONE REALLY ASKED YOU TO SHARE YOUR STORY? *WHAT WOULD YOU SAY?* IT'S NO SECRET THAT HOW YOU VIEW YOURSELF HAS A LOT TO DO WITH HOW OTHERS VIEW YOU. YOUR IMAGE IS EVERYTHING ON THE INSIDE THAT YOU CHOOSE TO PROJECT OUTWARD. AND IT COMES OUT IN ALL SORTS OF WAYS. YOUR SENSE OF STYLE, AVENUES OF SELF-EXPRESSION, LEVEL OF FITNESS, ATTENTION TO PERSONAL APPEARANCE, AND EVEN SPENDING HABITS ARE GREAT INDICATORS OF THE STUFF GOING ON INSIDE YOU. YOU ARE A COMPLEX CREATURE, AND NO SIMPLE THREE-PRONGED CONVERSATION STRATEGY WOULD EVER DO FOR COMMUNICATING THE "REAL" YOU. YOU ARE THE SUM OF ALL THESE THINGS AND MORE! AND WHILE OTHER PEOPLE'S PERCEPTION OF YOU MAY NOT BE YOUR NUMBER-ONE PRIORITY, THERE IS ONE PERSON WHO ABSOLUTELY NEEDS TO KNOW AND UNDERSTAND THE TOTAL, COMPLETE YOU, INCLUDING EVERY PART THAT ADDS TOGETHER TO MAKE THE WHOLE. NO, IT'S NOT YOUR SPOUSE OR FUTURE SPOUSE—IT'S *YOU!* IN A DECADE THAT IS FILLED TO THE MAX WITH TRANSITION AND STRESSFUL CHANGES, IT IS ABSOLUTELY CRITICAL THAT YOU TAKE ADEQUATE TIME TO REFLECT ON AND DEVELOP THE AREAS THAT COLLECTIVELY FORM *YOU* AS A HUMAN BEING. DON'T STAY IN THAT THREE-QUESTION SHALLOW END OF THE "YOU" POOL. IT IS INCREDIBLY EASY TO STAY STRESSED AND BUSY ALL THE TIME AND UNCONCERNED WITH KNOWING WHO YOU *REALLY* ARE. "FINDING YOURSELF" WAS A THING OF THE SIXTIES ANYWAY, WASN'T IT? BUT WITHOUT AN HONEST, ACCURATE UNDERSTANDING OF WHO YOU ARE TODAY, YOU WILL HAVE A MUCH HARDER TIME BECOMING WHO YOU WANT TO BE TOMORROW.

THE SKINNY ON THE 20s/THE
GENERATION
AT A GLANCE

The twentys

ACCORDING TO THE U.S. CENSUS BUREAU, there are approximately 38 million young adults between the ages of twenty and twenty-nine in the United States. You are part of a unique group, held together by shared experiences and a collective worldview. You differ greatly from your siblings in Generation X, especially in your attitudes toward success and money and in your general optimism about a brighter future. You're quite different from your Baby Boomer parents too. So who are you? Here are some thoughts on what defines this unique generation. . . .

SHARED EXPERIENCES

You're old enough to remember the dawn of the new millennium, and young enough that you can't remember a world without AIDS or MTV. You watched the first Gulf War on TV—it looked like a video game. School shootings, terrorism, and war broke your heart. Advances in technology allowed you to be the first generation raised with a global mind-set from the beginning. In fact, according to experts at Merrill Associates, twentys are actually the most racially diverse and global-minded generation ever.

SHARED VALUES

Possibly because of terrorism, war, and your awareness of the global economy, you are said to be a very caring and cause-driven group. Volunteerism is up, as is community involvement.

Twentys also seem to be more concerned with the *why* of their job and career, even more than the *what* they are doing. You place a very high value on making a difference with your life and with your job. According to a headhunter in Southern California, companies that used to offer great salaries and benefits packages are scrambling to add even more benefits like more vacation time and the freedom to work flexible hours. Of course, you'll keep the nice salaries and benefits as well, though, thank you. It's not that twentys are lazy or self-centered, it's just that their lives demand more flexibility since they're often involved in social issues and causes outside the workplace.

Many think it odd that twentys want to know a company's views on the environment and social-justice issues before agreeing to go to take the job. But that is one of your generation's distinguishing characteristics—a genuine desire for meaning and authenticity both in your own lives and in the lives of people and companies you interact with.

SHARED TRENDS

More and more twentys are moving back in with their parents after college. It may have been looked down on in the old days, but it's starting to become more of the norm now. Especially since this generation waits longer to get married and have children than any other group in history. One reason twentys don't leave the nest as early as previous generations did may be the increasing student-loan and credit-card debt people face today.

Twentys change jobs more often than previous generations. The job market right out of school is really tight, so many end up taking jobs that have nothing to do with their degree. It's okay, though, because they can just plan to work there a while until they decide what to do next.

Technology is a way of life these days. Twentys can't begin to understand why their parents have such a hard time setting their VCR. Mobility and convenience are top priorities. This generation prefers comfort and performance over hyped-out superficiality.

SHARED FUTURE

The twentys generation is poised to make a massive collective difference in the world. This generation's strong bond of shared experiences, values, and trends gives you everything you need to take on your shared future. You are on the edge of something big, ready for whatever challenges lie ahead. You've been raised up for such a time as this! • • • • • • • • • • •

THIS GENERATION WAITS LONGER TO GET MARRIED AND HAVE CHILDREN THAN ANY OTHER GROUP IN HISTORY \\\\\\\\\\\\\\\\\\\\\\\\\

DID YOU KNOW?

APPROACHING ADULTHOOD

Americans believe someone isn't a grown-up until they reach age 26. College-educated Americans surveyed chose an even higher age—between 28 and 29, according to a study of nearly 1,400 people over age 18.

(*Source: University of Chicago's National Opinion Research Center, as quoted by T.J. DeGroat in "Quarter Pounder," www.hatchmagazine.com/story.phtml?id=149.*)

WHO DO YOU WANT TO BE?

Deciding what to "do" with your life is one of the biggest questions you face as a twenty. It starts nagging you as soon as you graduate from high school—from deciding whether or not to go to college, to choosing a major if you do go, to heading off on a specific career path.

But what about a deeper issue—*who* do you want to *be* when you grow up? Here are some common answers given by twentys when asked the million-dollar question:

"I WANT TO BE SOMEONE IN AN AUTHENTIC RELATIONSHIP WITH GOD." If that is something you truly desire, it will take work. Humans have a natural tendency to want to mask their "real" selves, even with God. Having an authentic relationship with God requires time, energy, and a lot of heart.

"I WANT TO BE A PERSON OF INTEGRITY." Then you must make integrity a conscious, daily pursuit. It takes years to establish integrity, and it can be ripped away instantly with one bad decision. But even if you've messed up, don't be discouraged. Get back on the right path and ask God to help you.

"I WANT TO BE AN INTELLIGENT PERSON, AWARE OF WHAT'S GOING ON IN THE WORLD AROUND ME." Then read, read, read! Subscribe to a newspaper, and consider watching the six o'clock news instead of syndicated episodes of *Fear Factor* or *Friends* once in a while.

"I WANT TO BE BEAUTIFUL." *Note: For guys this would read, "I want to be hot."* Then outwardly you must do the best you can with what you've got. Inwardly, you must nurture the beauty of your heart.

"I WANT TO BE HEALTHY, FIT, AND ACTIVE." Then you simply must do all you already know to do but aren't doing for whatever reason you think up as an excuse.

You will never be the person you want to be unless you "do the time and pay the fine." So be sure you don't procrastinate too long. Identify the qualities you want to possess, figure out the best way to attain them, and then commit to doing whatever it takes to reach your goals.

TWENTYS TRANSITIONS

As you know, the twentys decade holds wide-sweeping change in just about every area of life. The rapid rate of transition can cause great stress, and the hectic lifestyle society demands leaves many twentys feeling isolated and alone. In reality, though, everyone else is just as screwed up as you are! Isn't that a comforting thought? Questions and doubts abound in everyone else's minds too.

Here's a lighthearted look at a few of the most common questions lurking behind each transition:

WHY CAN'T I JUST WEAR MY PAJAMA BOTTOMS?

SURVIVAL TO SUCCESS (MOVING FROM SCHOOL TO WORK)

Do I really have to be at work by 8:00 A.M. every single day? Why can't I just wear my pajama bottoms and a cap? How am I going to make rent this month? Has anyone ever died from a Ramen-noodles overdose? Why did I spend all that time and effort on my education when I still can't find a job?

SUCCESS TO SIGNIFICANCE (THE MID-TWENTYS CRISIS)

How can I find more balance in my life and make more time for the people and things that really matter? Am I making any difference in the world? Should I pay down my student loans or buy a new car? Is this the career path I should be taking? Why am I killing myself for a job that doesn't matter? Am I really who I should be on the path I should be at the time I should be?

SIGNIFICANCE TO SUFFICIENCY (ON THE THRESHOLD OF THIRTY)

Uh-oh! Am I supposed to have everything figured out by now? Am I giving enough of myself and my resources to things that matter? How can I plan for retirement? Should I settle down? get married? buy a house? get a dog? Are my parents going to be okay? How can I help them?

IMAGE QUOTES " "

Jerry Seinfeld to his elderly personal trainer: "How many sessions did my parents pay for?" Reply: "Not enough to make a man of you, daffodil!"

(Source: Seinfeld, NBC, episode 904)

WHO YOU ARE IN CHRIST

"ANYONE WHO BELONGS TO CHRIST HAS BECOME A NEW PERSON. THE OLD LIFE IS GONE; A NEW LIFE HAS BEGUN!" 2 CORINTHIANS 5:17 "YOU ARE A CHOSEN PEOPLE. YOU ARE ROYAL PRIESTS, A HOLY NATION, GOD'S VERY OWN POSSESSION." 1 PETER 2:9 "SEE HOW VERY MUCH OUR FATHER LOVES US, FOR HE CALLS US HIS CHILDREN, AND THAT IS WHAT WE ARE!" 1 JOHN 3:1 "JESUS SAID TO THE PEOPLE WHO BELIEVED IN HIM, 'YOU ARE TRULY MY DISCIPLES IF YOU REMAIN FAITHFUL TO MY TEACHINGS.'" JOHN 8:31

YOU UNIVERSITY
▶ FINDING YOU 101

There is much more to you than a quick one-sentence summary. You are a complex compilation of a million different facts, traits, and experiences. Knowing who you are and what you stand for in each of the following areas will help you achieve your life goals easier and faster. Spend some time examining the following parts of the whole:

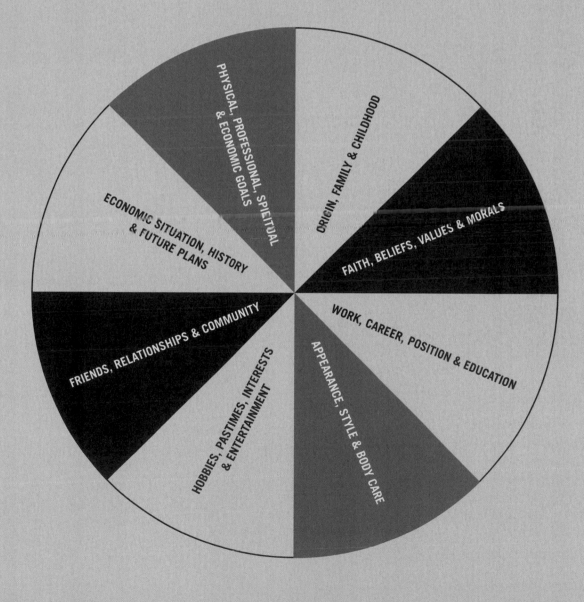

MAKE THE MOST OF LIFE ON THE GO»»»»»

WHETHER YOU ARE ON THE GO FOR WORK OR FUN, chances are you spend a significant amount of time away from home sweet home. Most twentys do! After all, this is the decade for carefree weekends, jam-packed business trips, and a busy life on the go. Here are some tips to help you make the most of it:

STAY CONNECTED»»»»

Coming home from a long, hard trip is draining. Boring meetings, uncomfortable shoes, insane security lines at the airport . . . your energy is zapped by the time you unlock the apartment door! Plugging back in with everyone at home can be the straw that breaks the exhausted camel's back.

But reconnecting after time away doesn't have to be hard. Just be honest with your loved ones. Tell them you're exhausted and that you really want to know all about their lives after you've had some rest. Then follow through and make time for them as soon as you can. Managing expectations from the get-go is the key. Many arguments and hurt feelings arise simply because people's expectations aren't realistic.

It is also much easier to reconnect in person if you never get disconnected in the first place.

TIP: *Try to make loved ones your top priority even on the road. A quick call or e-mail while you're traveling will go a long way toward smoothing out the "re-entry" process after the trip.*

GET YOUR ZZZZ'S»»»»

Switching time zones can be a killer when it comes to sleep habits. Waking up at four in the morning for a business meeting can really wreak havoc on a mind and body! Getting a good eight hours of sleep regardless of location or time zone is the key to avoiding a zombie-like appearance and mind-set. So whatever it takes to make yourself do it, be sure you get those allotted hours of quality rest. You will feel better, function better, and travel better if you do!

TIP: *Try using an over-the-counter sleep aid if you need extra help getting a full night's rest in another time zone.*

EXERCISE»»»»

Most high-quality hotels have nice fitness centers for people just like you. Make it a priority to maintain an active lifestyle even on the road. If a gym is not available, find other ways. Whatever you do, don't use travel as an excuse not to take care of your body!

TIP: *Travel with a workout DVD. And whenever there's a choice, walk to your destination instead of catching a ride.*

EAT RIGHT»»»»

What's still open after a red-eye flight? Not much! And the constant rushing from place to place can make it very difficult to eat healthy. But you can do it if you put your mind to it. Making good choices is the key.

TIP: *Always travel with a nutrition bar or healthy snack in your purse or briefcase for when you are stranded with nothing open or surrounded by bad options.*

CELL DEVELOPMENT

Sixty-one percent of Americans ages sixteen to twenty-nine would opt for a mobile phone over a landline, compared to 31 percent of those fifty or older.

(Source: IHRSA and the Ketchum Global Research Network)

DID YOU KNOW?

Although this list is far from exhaustive, it does offer a quick overview of important health issues and checkups every Twenty should be aware of. This list is simply for your personal health knowledge, though—you should get a checkup once a year and *always* consult your doctor about any health concerns!

EVEN TWENTYS NEED TO WATCH OUT FOR DANGER SIGNS IN THESE AREAS:

TESTICULAR CANCER Guys, this one is for you! And yes, this is what Lance Armstrong had! Testicular cancer is most common among men twenty-two to thirty-five years of age. With that in mind, it's important that you perform a self-examination at least once a month. To find out how to check yourself and what to look for, go to www.menweb.org/testican.

BREAST CANCER Ladies, the risk of breast cancer greatly increases once you turn thirty-five, but you should get into the habit of doing self-examinations while you're in your twenties. And if breast cancer runs in your family, you should be getting routine breast X-rays by the time you turn twenty-eight. For more information, visit www.cancer.org.

SKIN CANCER Remember all those days of frying yourself for the perfect tan? You know, back before the spray-on craze? Well, unfortunately a tan is not all you get from the golden sun. Doctors recommend checking your skin about once a month for any changes in moles, blemishes, or any other marks on your skin. Consult your doctor right away about any spots that change in size, shape, or color. And don't forget to use common sense and sunscreen whenever you're exposed to harmful ultraviolet rays.

CHOLESTEROL It's never too soon to be thinking about the health of your heart. Your doctor can check your cholesterol through a simple blood test. Find out whether your cholesterol is high or low and make whatever dietary or lifestyle adjustments your doctor recommends.

HERE ARE SOME TIPS ON IMPORTANT CHECKUPS:

EYE AND EAR EXAMS You should have your hearing and eyesight checked every one to two years!

DENTAL CHECKUPS Most doctors recommend visiting the dentist for a regular cleaning and checkup every six months.

PAP SMEARS Ladies, most doctors recommend you get a Pap smear test at least once every two years. And if you are sexually active or have been in the past, you should probably get tested every year. Find out more at www.4woman.gov.

Whenever you go in for any kind of checkup, don't be afraid to be honest with your doctor. He needs to know about any habits that might impact your health: playing sports, drinking alcohol, smoking, engaging in sexual activity, using drugs, etc. The more your doctor knows about you, the better equipped he'll be to help you manage your health and enjoy your twenties!

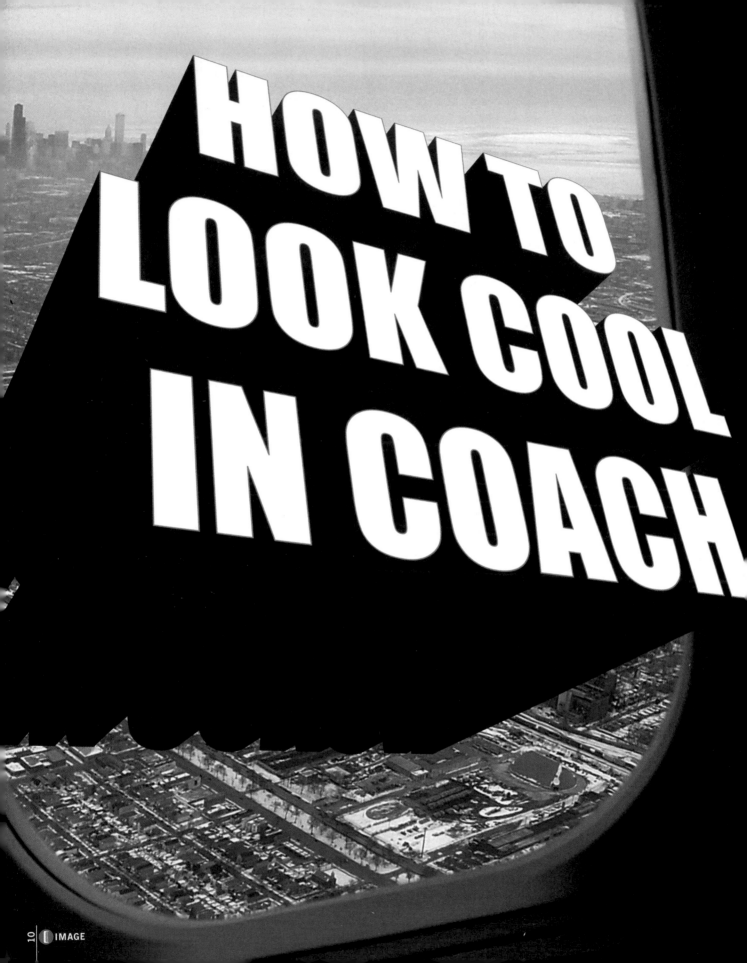

HOW TO LOOK COOL IN COACH

WE'VE ALL SEEN THEM. Harried, out-of-control travelers despised by everyone else on the plane. After a very late grand entrance, they traipse down the aisle with oversized carry-ons, slamming against shoulders as they pass. When they finally locate their places, there is no room in the overhead bin. The attendants have finished their final safety checks before the now-sweaty stress-buckets ever get settled in their last-row middle seats.

There are, on the other hand, much cooler passengers on board. You know—the mysterious ones that inspire your imagination and cause you to do a double-take when you spot them in the crowd. Here are a few things they all have in common:

SECURITY CHECKPOINTS ARE A SNAP. She talks on her cell phone all the way through the security line. At the last minute, she whips out her boarding pass and ID and eases through the checkpoint with amazing proficiency—laptop, shoes, belt, and cell in one container, jacket and change in another. How does she get everything off and out so fast? And how does she repack and get dressed again in mere seconds? Amazing!

PUNCTUALITY IS KEY. High flyers are always the first in line when their boarding group is called and overhead space abounds. By the time their seatmates arrive, they are enthralled in a very interesting book or magazine.

ONE BLACK ROLLING BAG DOES IT ALL. You never see these guys with bags hanging off every appendage. And your well-worn, much-loved backpack from college? Forget about it! Only the most professional black briefcase on wheels will do!

MEDIA AND PORTABLE ELECTRONICS ARE THE NAME OF THE GAME. Cell phone, laptop, PDA, iPod, personal DVD player, book, trendy magazines . . . they've got 'em all.

IMAGE MAKERS

What comes to other people's minds when they think of you? What image do you portray? Chances are, much of it has to do with their first impression of you. But that isn't the only factor. Here are a few others to keep in mind:

1. NON-VERBAL CUES AND THE WAY YOU CARRY YOURSELF

2. YOUR PERCEIVED CONFIDENCE LEVEL

3. DEGREE OF FRIENDLINESS

4. YOUR PERCEIVED AUTHENTICITY OR BELIEVABILITY

5. YOUR PERCEIVED COMPETENCE LEVEL

6. YOUR SPEECH PATTERNS *(CLEAR OR MUDDLED? ACCENT? PROPER GRAMMAR?)*

7. THE WAY YOU TYPICALLY DRESS

8. YOUR PERCEIVED LEVEL OF INTEREST IN THEM

8. THE PASSION YOU EXUDE ABOUT A GIVEN SUBJECT

TOP 10 SIGNS
YOU ARE NOT HOME ENOUGH

1. You accidentally dial "9" first when dialing from home.

2. Your "neighbors" are whoever you happen to sit by today.

3. You never use the same towel twice.

4. All your plants are either dead or plastic.

5. Your idea of vacationing involves staying home.

6. The airport security people know you by name.

7. You are one of the few Americans who actually know what TSA stands for.

8. You expect a free *USA Today* outside your door at home.

9. You're given a guest card when you attend your home church.

10. You see your own face on the milk carton.

65% POLYESTER
35% COTTON-COTON
MADE IN BANGLADESH
FABRIQUE AU BANGLADESH

IMAGE MAKERS

16½
42 CM

QUIZ: DO YOU HAVE *Style*?

1. IT'S SATURDAY MORNING AND YOU NEED TO RUN TO THE STORE FOR A QUICK ITEM. DO YOU–

(a) throw on a cap and sweats and leave without brushing your teeth?

(b) brush your hair or put it in a ponytail, grab some jeans, and rush out hoping no one will see you?

(c) fix your hair and put on makeup or quickly shave in case you see someone you know?

2. YOU NEED NEW SHOES. DO YOU–

(a) buy whatever is affordable and decent in your size (trying them on is optional)?

(b) try on several pairs at a couple of stores until you find the pair that you think will be comfortable, durable, *and* fashionable?

(c) buy a pair here and there, intending to go back later and return the ones you don't want to keep?

3. PARIS HILTON JUST WALKED INTO YOUR FRIEND'S BIRTHDAY PARTY. YOU WONDER . . .

(a) *Isn't Paris the capital of France?*

(b) *What's she doing here? Am I getting* Punk'd?

(c) *Where on earth does she get those clothes? How does she manage to keep the bow in that little purse dog's hair?*

If you answered (a) for all three questions, you've got bigger things on your mind than style. You may see your style as a non-issue. But did you know that not caring is a certain style in and of itself? You're one of a kind, so be your own unique self!

If all your answers were (b), you have a classic sense of style. You play it safe, yet care about the image you portray. Be sure you don't overspend on last year's trends. Just be you—you are, after all, a classic!

If you picked (c) for all three answers, you're one of those people who guessed (c) for all the hard questions on the SATs, aren't you? Not only that, but you are a person of high style. You smell a trend a mile away and are usually the one who introduces it to your circle. Be sure you don't choose *fabricated* over *original*. Just be yourself—you're fabulous!

DECIPHERING THE SECRET DRESS CODE OF THE AFTER-SCHOOL WORLD

After years of rolling out of bed, brushing your teeth, and hurrying out the door in sweats and a baseball cap, your first "real" job can be a rude awakening. The sheer torture of having to rise before dawn should be punishment enough for having summers off during the last four to eight years, but it's only the beginning. Compounding the problem is the crazy jargon everyone speaks when talking about what to wear. It's like they have some private dictionary or reference book that new recruits are forbidden to see. Every time there's a party, meeting, or event, they spring a new dress code on you. It can literally take years to crack the secret code. And by the time you figure it out, none of the clothes in your present wardrobe will even be in style anymore!

Maybe this is considered insider trading, but here is a classified list of definitions to help you look your appropriate best on every occasion:

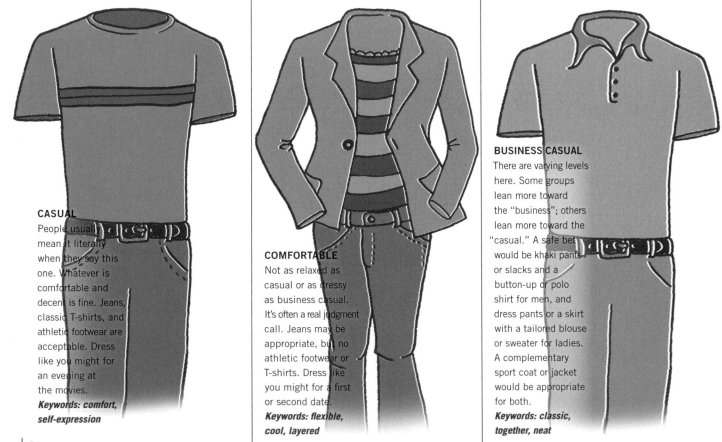

CASUAL
People usually mean it literally when they say this one. Whatever is comfortable and decent is fine. Jeans, classic T-shirts, and athletic footwear are acceptable. Dress like you might for an evening at the movies.
Keywords: comfort, self-expression

COMFORTABLE
Not as relaxed as casual or as dressy as business casual. It's often a real judgment call. Jeans may be appropriate, but no athletic footwear or T-shirts. Dress like you might for a first or second date.
Keywords: flexible, cool, layered

BUSINESS CASUAL
There are varying levels here. Some groups lean more toward the "business"; others lean more toward the "casual." A safe bet would be khaki pants or slacks and a button-up or polo shirt for men, and dress pants or a skirt with a tailored blouse or sweater for ladies. A complementary sport coat or jacket would be appropriate for both.
Keywords: classic, together, neat

DRESSY CASUAL
This is just a little dressier than business casual. No polos or sweaters, just tailored button-ups and nice slacks or a skirt.
Keywords: tailored, buttoned-up

PROFESSIONAL
No-holds-barred, all-the-stops-pulled, full-on suit attire for both genders. Put it all out there—dress to the nines!
Keywords: serious, polished, powerful

COCKTAIL
More elegant than professional wear for early evening occasions. Dark suits for men and short dressy dresses *(like the classic "little black dress")* or coordinated separates for ladies.
Keyword: stylish, chic, classy

SEMI-FORMAL
This is a toughie. Daytime events are a little less dressy than nighttime occasions. A dark suit for him and a short dress or tailored suit for her should do nicely.
Keywords: pretty/ handsome, elegant

FORMAL OR BLACK TIE
Pretend you're going to the prom. Tuxes for men and long dresses or eveningwear separates for ladies. A cocktail dress may do in some cases.
Keywords: mega-dressy, refined, Oscars red carpet

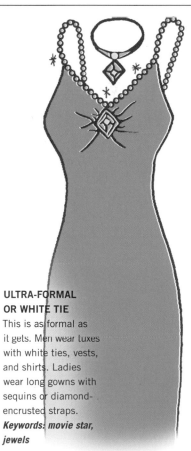

ULTRA-FORMAL OR WHITE TIE
This is as formal as it gets. Men wear tuxes with white ties, vests, and shirts. Ladies wear long gowns with sequins or diamond-encrusted straps.
Keywords: movie star, jewels

BASICS FOR EVERY
PROFESSIONAL TWENTY'S WARDROBE

These years are not exactly famous for glitz, glamour, or excessive monetary gain. You could easily blow your whole budget on clothes alone. Carefully choosing quality fabric and classic styles that never go out of date can help you make the most of your fashion purchases.

You don't have to have mounds of clothing for every season or occasion. Just a few well-selected pieces will do:

❶ PROFESSIONAL SUIT

❶ LITTLE BLACK DRESS
(GIRLS ONLY, PLEASE!)

❷ PAIRS OF BLACK PANTS
(ONE CASUAL AND ONE A LITTLE MORE DRESSY)

❺ FITTED SHIRTS

❶ BLAZER

❷ PAIRS OF TAN OR KHAKI PANTS

❷ CASUAL SHIRTS (IN CASE YOUR COMPANY OPTS FOR CASUAL FRIDAYS!)

❷ PAIRS OF BLACK SHOES (ONE FOR EVERYDAY AND ONE FOR MORE FORMAL OCCASIONS)

SOMETIMES IT'S BETTER IF YOU JUST *SHUT UP!*

IT'S BETTER IF YOU JUST SHUT UP . . . when you *really* don't know what you're talking about. Some of us tend to want to give an opinion about everything. Well, before you get all "Bill O'Reilly" on someone, make sure you're not simply talking to hear yourself talk.

IT'S BETTER IF YOU JUST SHUT UP . . . when you know that speaking is only going to make things worse. Use your common sense, people. You know when your words will hurt. Walk away from the situation. Think about green and yellow fireflies. Pinch yourself. Do whatever you have to do to take the high road and remain silent. Remember, words are impossible to take back.

IT'S BETTER IF YOU JUST SHUT UP . . . when you're the only one in the room. Yeah, people who talk to themselves only *think* it's healthy.

IT'S BETTER IF YOU JUST SHUT UP . . . if you're the only one talking. Don't you hate it when people talk and talk and talk and give no attention to the fact that everyone in the room is trying desperately to ignore them? For goodness' sake, just be quiet!

IT'S BETTER IF YOU JUST SHUT UP . . . when you're wearing headphones. No more "Hey, I love this song!!!" in the middle of Borders.

IT'S BETTER IF YOU JUST SHUT UP . . . when with each passing phrase you dig a hole deeper than you'll ever be able to fill. Shhhh. Come here. Let me whisper in your ear: Shut up!

IT'S BETTER IF YOU JUST SHUT UP...
when deep down you think it'd be better to be quiet. Sometimes you just have to go with your gut. If you think your story is too personal to share—it probably is. If you think it's going to be uncomfortable to "open up" in front a large audience, imagine what the large audience must be thinking.

IT'S BETTER IF YOU JUST SHUT UP...
when someone is giving you a compliment. It may be hard to hear nice things about yourself–it's difficult for all of us. But you can handle a little self-gratification once in a while. So just shut up 'til they finish telling you you're wonderful—then say thank you. Then shut up again.

FASHION *NEVERS* FOR BUSINESS

NEVER appear sloppy or unkempt. Keep hair trimmed out of your eyes, and avoid the frumpy look.

NEVER wear revealing or too-tight clothing. Ladies, make sure your skirt length isn't too short. Men, be sure your suit jacket isn't too tight.

NEVER start the day in wrinkles. Take special care when traveling, and allow extra time to iron in the morning.

NEVER be the least-formally dressed person in the room. It is always better to be overdressed than underdressed.

NEVER wear tennis shoes to any business function unless you will be playing sports.

TAKE THE STAIRS INSTEAD OF THE ELEVATOR.
Or at least climb three or four flights and then ride the rest of the way.

PARK AT THE END OF THE LOT or at the top of the parking deck.

STRETCH DURING EACH COMMERCIAL SET while watching television.

TIGHTEN AND RELEASE GLUTEUS MAXIMUS muscles every time you are standing in a checkout line—just try not to make this too obvious.

CATCH UP WITH FRIENDS BY GOING FOR A WALK together rather than sharing a meal.

MOVE UP AND DOWN ON YOUR TIPTOES the whole two minutes you brush your teeth.

ADD ACTIVITY TO YOUR DAY

LASTING WAYS TO MAKE A GOOD
· · · · · · · · · · · · · · · · · · ·FIRST IMPRESSION

The old adage is true: You never get a second chance to make a first impression. If you happen to be tired from staying up too late or are in a stressed-out tizzy over some looming deadline, big deal! A new coworker or acquaintance has no way of knowing you're just having an "off day."

The reason you didn't smile when you met them could be as innocent and understandable as the blinding pain from a migraine you had at that moment. But they may walk away with the impression that you're arrogant, unfriendly, or worse. And you will have an uphill battle trying to recover the ground you lost in that one instant . . . not only with whomever you just met, but with everyone they talk to about you!

First impressions are indeed lasting and often quite powerful. Make yours a positive one.

ESTABLISH AND HOLD EYE CONTACT. Looking someone directly in the eyes communicates confidence in yourself and interest in the person you're meeting. Avoiding eye contact gives the impression of disinterest or even dishonesty.

SMILE—IF ONLY FOR A MOMENT. Everyone has days when they do not feel like smiling. They don't want to be a fake or a hypocrite, so they end up going through the day with a serious scowl or pained look. Even if you really do have a noble and just cause for sadness, anger, or pain, set it aside for a second and swing a smile toward someone you're meeting for the first time. It is sure to go far and serve you well. Don't be phony, walking around like everything is hunky-dory all the time, but forcing a smile from time to time does not make you a hypocrite.

DON'T FORGET THE ALL-IMPORTANT HANDSHAKE. Greetings in North America are fairly uniform. There is no reason for you to ever botch one! Remember that a solid, firm handshake combined with sincere eye contact demonstrates confidence and respect.

REPEAT THE PERSON'S NAME. Immediately using new names in a sentence will help you remember them later. And the person you meet will be more likely to remember you, too, if you show enough interest to speak their name out loud.

PLAN OUT YOUR APPEARANCE AHEAD OF TIME. If you know you will be meeting someone for the first time, take special care when choosing your outfit, and for goodness' sake, shower, brush your teeth, and spend a little time on your hair. Pop in a strong mint to eliminate any stinky cells. It may sound elementary, but how many times have you met someone and wondered why he looked so sloppy or still smelled like yesterday's coffee?

RESEARCH COMMON INTERESTS. If time and opportunity exist, do a little sleuthing to find out what likes, dislikes, or history you may share with the person you are about to meet. Make a mental list of subjects you could bring up for easy conversation.

BE THE REAL, AUTHENTIC YOU . . . and do what you can to project the best version!

PUDGY POPULATION

The percentage of people who are obese doubles from the teen years to the mid-twentys, according to a study that tracked almost ten thousand people. About 22 percent of twentys are obese, which means they are roughly thirty pounds over a healthy weight. About half of them were obese as teenagers.

(Source: "Obesity Explodes from Teens to 20s," as cited on www.intelihealth.com, October 13, 2003)

DIGITAL BEAUTY

According to a New York City photographer whose retouching service works with advertising agencies, 100% of fashion photos are re-touched. Eyes and teeth are whitened, and skin and hair are flattened. Noses and hips are narrowed, while lips are thickened out.

(Source: "Pretty Unreal," Current Health, January 2005; http://medialit.med.sc.edu/ pretty_unreal.htm)

THE EYE OF THE STORM

YOUR BODY'S CALM BEFORE (AND AFTER) THE TWENTYS DECADE

THE TWENTYS OFFER A BRIEF RESPITE between the growth and the decline of your body. Your twentys are as good as it gets! The traumatic effects of puberty are finally ending. Gone (or at least *almost* gone!) are the zits, squeaks, and body morphing of adolescence. The storm of emotional and hormonal changes (other than unsightly beginnings of back hair on men) is rolling to a nice, soothing end. Good riddance!

And that downward spiral into the body's dreaded thirty-plus accelerated aging process? Not here yet! Right now you are in the prime of your life. Energy, performance, and stamina are at their best. Long live the twentys!

Unfortunately, though, the twentys do not "live long." As you approach thirty, your metabolism begins to slow and the prime of life begins to fade. But take heart! If you establish a healthy lifestyle now, you will reap solid benefits for all the decades to come.

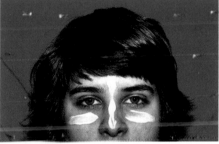

LOSE IT FOR LIFE!

This slogan for New Life Ministries' weight-management program is so fitting for the twentys decade. If you are among the millions of Americans who weigh more than what is recommended, now is absolutely the time to make positive changes for better health.

As you get older, your metabolism begins to slow and losing weight becomes increasingly more difficult. As hard as it may be now to shed those extra pounds—and keep them off—it will only get harder with time.

Countless psychologists, physicians, and other experts have devised a thousand different ways to lose weight. But no plan in the world will work until you decide to create a lifelong habit of healthy choices. Wholehearted determination breeds success.

EXERCISE.

Regardless of weight, everybody needs daily exercise. The ten years between twenty and thirty are filled with sometimes overwhelming busyness, transition, and stress. For many, it really is hard to find time to work out. In fact, if you are hoping to "find" time for exercise, you might as well give up now. It's not there unless you make it a part of your lifestyle!

A consistent routine of cardio and weight training will help fight heart disease, stroke, diabetes, and a host of other problems that may be lurking around the corner. Sorry, guys, but the intense thumb workout from your Xbox doesn't count. And, girls, nine hours of mall shopping doesn't count either. Sorry.

PROTECT YOUR SKIN.

One of the most common (and stupid!) mistakes spring breakers make every year is the painful sunburn they bring home. If you think the burning, itching, and peeling is bad, wait until it develops into skin cancer or wrinkles down the road!

To keep nice, tight, healthy skin as you age, use sunscreen with at least 15 SPF every time you are exposed to the sun. Cleanse, moisturize, and protect your skin now for brighter, healthier, and smoother skin throughout your lifetime. Drink lots of water, too, so you don't look like a shriveled-up prune in later years.

Make a point now to *not* snooze through this decade in the eye of the storm. Use it to establish healthy habits and a lifestyle of good choices. Then you can stand confident, even in the midst of the gale-force winds of change that await you in the coming years!

Stress is a daily companion for many twentys. Early years include college finals, post-graduation job searches, and living on your own for the first time. Then comes the inner turmoil and conflict of what some have so cleverly called the "quarter-life crisis." And there's no denying the stress of the slippery slope toward the milestone of turning thirty. This is most definitely a stress-*full* decade!

COMMON CULPRITS

Sometimes it seems like every decision is a huge one—like every day brings a new life-changing choice with one right answer and fifty million wrong ones. *What am I going to do with my life?* is one of the most common stress activators of this decade. The question echoes relentlessly within many of us like some sort of twentys mantra.

And we wonder not only *What am I going to do with the rest of my life?* but also *Who am I going to do it with?* The issue of romance and lifelong love nearly drives many of us bonkers. Those who enter into meaningful relationships experience the ups and downs of it all. And those who don't find their soulmate soon enough must deal with the many highs and lows of the search for a significant other.

Transition is another major stress contributor. Unfortunately, the old cliché about the only constant being change is all too true during this stage of life. Twentys must adjust to moving away from old friends, learning to be an independent adult, switching jobs, losing loved ones, and changing family roles.

SYMPTOMS

At any given time, one of these factors could overwhelm you with the sense of having more than you can handle. Add several of these factors together, and the stress level can become out of control, often showing itself in other ways. Some symptoms include headaches, insomnia, fatigue, changes in appetite, backaches, and skin problems. If left unmanaged, greater issues like heart health and mental illness can arise.

If you are chronically tired, plagued by sleeplessness, or constantly sick with any bug that comes through town, you may be overly stressed. Other telltale signs include sudden weight gain or loss and a sense of dread or hopelessness.

RELIEF

It's a good thing we're so young and vibrant when all this stress comes along! A healthy lifestyle including regular exercise, rest, and time with friends, along with balanced nutrition and adequate water intake, can do wonders for a stressed-out body.

One of the easiest and most effective ways to relieve stress is to reduce the amount of it you allow in the first place. Recognizing limits, drawing boundaries, and sticking to them are all signs of maturity. Resist the urge to take on more than you can realistically handle at work, at church, and with friends and significant others. If you don't want to choke, don't bite off more than you can chew!

The important thing is to get a handle on the stress that threatens to choke out the fun of being a twenty. This can be the time of your life. Make sure you enjoy it!

> Sometimes it seems like every decision is a huge one—like every day brings a new life-changing choice...

DOs

FIND A HOT TUB.

BUY A PUNCHING BAG.

EXERCISE FURIOUSLY.

TAKE A CHILL PILL.

PRAY WITHOUT CEASING.

TALK IT OUT WITH YOUR LOVED ONES.

ACKNOWLEDGE AT ONCE THAT YOU CAN'T DO EVERYTHING.

PLAY SOFT MUSIC AND LIGHT CANDLES.

BREAK LARGE TASKS INTO MANAGEABLE, BITE-SIZED PIECES.

DRINK IN THE NICE, FRESH AIR OUTDOORS.

STRESSED?

DON'Ts

EAT A TUB OF ICE CREAM.

PUNCH YOUR ROOMMATE.

DRIVE FURIOUSLY.

RESORT TO ANY OTHER PILLS.

EAT WITHOUT CEASING.

TAKE IT OUT ON YOUR LOVED ONES.

TRY TO DO EVERYTHING AT ONCE.

PLAY IN THE ROAD OR LIGHT ROMAN CANDLES.

BITE YOUR FINGERNAILS.

GET SLOPPY DRUNK.

DID YOU KNOW?

STRESSED OUT

"41% of today's 20- to 29-year-olds say they feel either quite a bit of pressure or almost more stress than they can bear."

(Source: Knowledge Networks quoted in Advertising Age)

HEY GOOD LOOKIN', WHATCHA GOT COOKIN'?

Americans ages twenty-four to thirty-five average only five home-cooked meals a week.

(Source: Boyce Thompson, "X Marks the Spot," Builder, February 2001)

Do you want to have the *it* quality everyone talks about? Of course you do. Try on these fifteen character traits for a personality makeover. Even if you master just half of these qualities, you'll be well on your way to becoming dashing and intoxicating. Heck, you'll be totally killer —we just know it!

GET IT!
15 QUALITIES TODAY'S TWENTY MUST HAVE

1 BE TENACIOUS

Pushovers end up being lifelong servers at truck stops. *(Not that there's anything wrong with that!)*

2 BE RADICAL

Change something. Be different and out of the box.

3 BE SENSITIVE

Softhearted people rule the world. *(Not really, but they are really nice to be around.)*

4 BE CONFIDENT

You know you got it in ya. Exude it, baby!

5 BE FLEXIBLE

No, not like a gymnast. Although, sometimes that certainly helps.

6 BE CREATIVE

Life is competitive— and those who make it more interesting go to the top.

7 BE OPTIMISTIC

Always anticipate whipped cream and cherries. No really, look on the bright side.

8 BE PASSIONATE

If you love what you do, you'll do what you do better.

9 BE PEACEFUL

The person who looks for a peaceful resolution to any conflict is wise. *(Not always popular—but really, really wise.)*

10 BE HONEST

Liars burn in hell. That's what my dad always told me.

11 BE COMPASSIONATE

Think about how your actions influence the world around you.

12 BE HUMBLE

Those who have it don't flaunt it.

13 BE SIMPLE

Don't make life any more complicated than it already is.

14 BE LOVABLE

Just like a cute little puppy. Human affection is one of God's greatest gifts.

15 BE FREE

The non-free end up confused, depressed, and unsatisfied with life.

7 HABITS OF HAPPY TWENTYS

❶ SET, TRACK, AND ACHIEVE PERSONAL GOALS.
Whether they're reading the entire Shakespeare collection, buying a house, losing weight, or collecting a thousand pogs, happy twentys put their hearts and minds into something and don't give up until they accomplish it.

❷ CULTIVATE A TEACHABLE SPIRIT.
Happy twentys learn from mistakes (their own and others'), from friends and mentors, and even from ill-intended criticism. Instead of getting defensive, they listen carefully and look for ways to improve.

❸ MAKE HEALTHY CHOICES.
The happiest twentys habitually make good decisions about food, rest, exercise, and boundaries. It may not come naturally to these individuals at first, but their determination leads them to a place where the good choice is obvious, if not altogether easy.

❹ PLUG INTO PERSONAL COMMUNITY.
The most contented, well-adjusted twentys are surrounded by a network of caring loved ones. They live in community with this personal network, sharing burdens, concerns, joy, and laughter on a regular basis.

❺ SPEND DAILY TIME WITH GOD.
Authentic, active faith in the living God spurs happy twentys toward spending quality time with him each day. They are motivated to do this by love, not by rules—out of a desire for fellowship and not out of fear.

❻ FIND A JOB TO BELIEVE IN AND ENJOY.
Getting up and going to work doesn't have to be drudgery—it can be a delight. Follow your passion to the kind of workplace that lets it grow. A happy twenty is a productive twenty.

❼ INVEST IN OTHERS.
Happy twentys know what it means to live beyond themselves. They mentor, teach, disciple, or volunteer with a pure heart for serving others. They take an interest in the world around them and long to make a difference in people's lives.

TIPS FOR CREATING SPACE TASTEFULLY

Buy or make decorative boxes in varying shapes and patterns. Arrange them in unused areas of open space.

Purchase or make a loft bed, and create a work or study area underneath. Or place a futon there for guests to use.

Use a trunk as a coffee table. Extra linens and other things can be stored within.

Place your TV and other electronics on pieces that double as storage cabinets.

Use every area of height by placing shelves or stackable crates along the wall. Attractive baskets can keep the area clutter free and still functional.

IMAGE QUOTES

"I must lead a sheltered life because none of the women in the ads look like anyone I know. No one sits around looking like this in the places I go, either. . . . I've never seen a guy put his hand in his pocket like this either except in an ad for a suit."

—Andy Rooney,
CBS News correspondent

DECORATE
YOUR DOMAIN—*EVEN DORMS & APARTMENTS NEED LOVE*

Dorm and apartment living leave much to be desired. Small spaces equal big frustrations for many. And those stark white walls? Puh-leeese! Don't go through this decade of fun in a boring environment like that! You aren't a boring person, are you? Why shouldn't your home reflect the super-cool, tré-hip guy or gal you are? Liven it up; make it yours! Own it, baby—whether you *own* it or not! Here's how:

SCHEME IN COLOR ■ ■ ■

A well-thought-out color palate can make all the difference in a dorm room or apartment. Ask any kindergartener and he can tell you his favorite color. From the time we are little tykes, our appreciation of color is developing and evolving. It's natural for us to be drawn to certain colors or combinations that reflect our personality, evoke memories of yesteryear, or inspire our mood.

Go with that. Just because the Fab Five say it's cool or a designer on TLC happens to use it on every episode of *Trading Spaces* doesn't mean you have to like it. Choose a color scheme that is uniquely you. You'll be much happier with it for much longer if you do.

Now, after you've identified your color scheme of choice, don't go overboard. Walk that fine line between cool and tacky very carefully. Choose one major color and then use it as an accent throughout the room. It will be the unifying theme your eye keeps coming back to, no matter where it roams.

PATTERNS WORK MAGIC ■ ■ ■

Vertical lines create the illusion of extended height, while complex patterns with multiple colors, directions, and shapes may overwhelm a small area. Small prints work nicely in small spaces. Save the big sweeping patterns for large living areas.

PRACTICAL MAKE3 PERFECT ■ ■ ■

Now that it doesn't look like the crayon box threw up in your living quarters and the mixed patterns don't make you want to poke your eyes out, let's talk functionality. Many twentys don't have huge homes with three-car garages. Those are normally reserved for people in their forties at least. So you need to maximize every square inch of your space for self-expression *and* self-preservation.

Express yourself with fun, unique accessories and furniture. Preserve yourself with smart storage, accessible hideaways, and affordable solutions. Make sure every piece of furniture serves a purpose. Make sure the space in every corner, under every table or bed, and in every nook and cranny is being used efficiently.

DON'T FORGET THE DETAILS ■ ■ ■

Pay attention to the little details that make a big difference. Dress up older pieces of furniture with fresh paint, stencils, or fabric. If you live in a building that prohibits major changes, consider using starch and water to harmlessly hang lightweight fabric on the walls instead of wallpaper or paint. Re-cover old throw pillows and strategically place an afghan or blanket for a touch of style, warmth, and love. ■

GRIEF & TRAUMA 911

As uncomfortable as it is to think about, you may experience major losses or trauma during the twentys years. Grandparents or other loved ones may pass away. Traumatic accidents or prolonged illnesses may shake your world. Whether you face the death of a loved one, the loss of a relationship, or even unfulfilled dreams, it is crucial to take time to grieve properly.

Of course, not everyone will be forced to face the harsh realities of life yet. But even if you are one of those fortunate souls, keep reading. Chances are you know someone who will travel the painful road of grief and recovery.

STAGES OF GRIEF

Everyone grieves differently, and every situation is unique. But Swiss-born psychiatrist Elisabeth Kübler-Ross identified five common stages of grief: denial, resentment, bargaining, depression, and acceptance. These are not necessarily linear or chronological—a person can actually be in more than one stage at a time or jump around between them for a while. There is no strict timeline or easy recipe for moving through the process, but being aware of the common stages may help eliminate some of the fear and worry associated with this time of sorrow.

WHAT TO EXPECT

The emotions, tears, and mood swings you may encounter can be frightening, especially if you've never dealt with anything so severe before. You may think you're going mental when intense longings or waves of pain shoot through your heart. But rest easy, friend, and know that it's normal and even healthy to experience sudden bouts of crying, emotional numbness, or changes in outlook. Insomnia, guilt, the desire to withdraw, dull or hollow aching pain in the abdomen or chest area, and decreased energy or concentration levels are all very normal, especially in the early stages of grief.

It's normal to even feel angry with God from time to time after facing a traumatic experience. It's good and appropriate to talk to him about whatever you're feeling. Read the book of Job for a good example.

HOW TO COPE

As you move through the stages of the grieving process, try not to force yourself to "forget it and move on" right away. Permit yourself to feel the pain and admit the sorrow. Talk about it with friends or a support group. In the early days, it can be helpful to share stories about how it used to be or to retell the events that led up to the traumatic moment of death or loss. It's very important to eat right and exercise even in the midst of grief too. Emotional struggles can really zap your energy—and right when you need it most. When you're too tired or lethargic or hungry or full, you don't have all the tools you need to press on. Also, be sure to plan ahead as special anniversaries or holidays approach. Don't hesitate to lean on family and friends during those especially painful times throughout the year. Do whatever you can to build up your resolve to keep on keeping on as hard days approach. Spend extra time in the comforting Scriptures, and recruit your closest friends to pray extra hard for you.

On paper, the grief-recovery process can seem easy, straightforward, and rather sterile. But it can be overwhelming when you find yourself in the middle of a traumatic loss. The hard truth is that death and loss are part of life and love. You can't experience one without the other. But you can at least do your best to prepare for the heartache and learn all you can before the worst hits. Above all else, the best thing you can possibly do to prepare is to build a solid foundation of faith and a strong relationship with Christ now.

HELPING OTHERS GRIEVE

There is rarely anything more difficult than seeing someone you love in pain or deep sorrow. You may feel a combined sense of helplessness and awkwardness that leaves you at a loss as to what to say or do. You may find yourself hovering and fussing until you smother the poor person who is grieving. Or you may be tempted to flee the scene altogether. But your loved one needs you desperately during times of great suffering. Here are some tips for helping others through the grieving process:

HELPFUL, SUPPORTIVE DOs

DO SHOW UP. Just being there speaks more than any brilliant, comforting word or Scripture you spout off. Don't stay away just because you don't have anything to say.

DO EMBRACE THE SILENCE. Some of the most precious, helpful times you'll share are those spent in silence.

DO LISTEN MORE THAN YOU TALK. Allow your grieving friend to talk about his loss. Encourage him to share memories and stories. Don't force it, though. Just let him know you're ready to listen if and when he's ready to talk.

DO OFFER PRACTICAL HELP. Look around and notice things that need doing. Make calls, help with arrangements, offer to babysit, house-sit or pet-sit, cook a meal, or run an errand.

DO REMEMBER HOLIDAYS AND ANNIVERSARIES. Your loved one may experience the heaviest sadness and most intense sorrow when special days are near. Simply acknowledging that you remember will bring more comfort than you can imagine.

DO MAKE NEW MEMORIES. Introduce new friends and activities. Do something different or go somewhere new. Fill the empty spaces with happy times.

HURTFUL, COUNTERPRODUCTIVE DON'Ts

DON'T SPEAK IN CLICHÉS. It is not even remotely helpful to say dumb things like, "He's in a much better place" or "You'll get over this with time" or "It's all for the best."

DON'T TRY TO FIX IT. Honestly, there is nothing you can say or do that will make everything all better, so don't even try.

DON'T MAKE COMPARISONS. For goodness' sake, don't talk about a previous loss you've experienced or what someone else is going through. That minimizes or discounts rather than validates.

DON'T ENCOURAGE OR ENABLE BAD CHOICES. Watch for excessive weight loss or gain, evidence of substance abuse, or suicidal tendencies. These can be very serious signs that your loved one is not coping in a healthy way. Encourage them to seek professional help if manifestations of grief seem out of control. *(Call 1-800-New-Life or visit www.newlife.com for an excellent referral network.)*

DON'T MAKE JUDGMENT CALLS. No matter how well-intentioned you are, suggesting that your loved one should not be grieving or should be over it by now is never helpful.

DON'T RUSH THE HEALING. All you really want is for your loved one to feel better and enjoy life again. That's natural. But don't rush it. Allow time to grieve. Give her space when she needs it. Acknowledge the grief even months later and ask how she's doing when everyone else seems to have forgotten her heartbreak.

RELATIO

RELATIONSHIPS—AN INTRODUCTION

WHEN TWENTYS ARE ASKED TO IDENTIFY THE MOST IMPORTANT THINGS IN LIFE, RELATIONSHIPS RANK IN THEIR TOP FIVE FELT NEEDS. TWENTYS WANT TO KNOW, WHO WILL BE MY FRIENDS? HOW WILL I FIND SOMEONE TO LOVE ME? WHEN I DO, WILL THEY LOVE ME FOR ME? WHY CAN'T I GET ALONG WITH MY PARENTS? RELATIONSHIPS ARE INCREDIBLY IMPORTANT TO LIFE, AND THEY PROVIDE US WITH SOME OF THE RICHEST DRAMA WE WILL EVER EXPERIENCE. GETTING A GRIP ON RELATIONSHIPS IS VITAL FOR EVERY TWENTY. RELATIONSHIP ADVICE IS EVERYWHERE. WE FIND IT IN MAGAZINES, ON THE RADIO AND TV, IN MOVIES, AND FROM OUR FRIENDS. BUT THERE ARE FEW RESOURCES THAT OFFER TWENTYS GODLY INSIGHT FOR DEVELOPING THE NECESSARY SKILLS TO BOTH SURVIVE AND ENJOY THE RELATIONSHIPS OF LIFE. THAT'S WHAT THIS CHAPTER IS ALL ABOUT, AND IT STARTS NOW. DO YOU EVER FEEL AWKWARD TRYING TO RELATE TO OLDER, MORE EXPERIENCED COLLEAGUES AT WORK? WHAT ABOUT YOUR DATING RELATIONSHIPS? EVER FEEL UNSURE WHETHER YOU'RE *GOING* OUT OR JUST *HANGING* OUT? DO YOU EVER WONDER WHAT MARRIAGE IS TRULY ALL ABOUT AND WHETHER YOU'VE GOT WHAT IT TAKES TO MAKE IT LAST? AND THEN THERE ARE YOUR PARENTS. THAT ONE WORD CAN SPARK AN ERUPTION OF RESENTMENT OR AFFECTION FROM JUST ABOUT ANY TWENTY. RELATIONSHIPS ARE CENTRAL TO LIFE AND TO THE PLANS AND PURPOSES OF GOD. BEFORE HE RETURNED TO HEAVEN, JESUS SAID THAT BELIEVERS ARE TO SPEND THEIR LIVES MAKING DISCIPLES (MATTHEW 28:19-20). YOU SHOW JESUS TO THE WORLD THROUGH YOUR RELATION-SHIPS. SO LEARNING PROPER RELATIONSHIP SKILLS ISN'T JUST A GOOD IDEA—IT HAS AN IMPACT ON ETERNITY. HEALTHY RELATIONSHIPS TEACH YOU ABOUT YOURSELF AND HOLD YOU ACCOUNTABLE TO THE HIGHER CALLING ON YOUR LIFE. YOU NEED FRIENDS WHO WILL CHALLENGE YOU TO BECOME MORE AND MORE LIKE CHRIST. THE BIBLE SAYS THAT GOD LOVED THE WORLD SO MUCH THAT HE SENT HIS SON TO GIVE HIS LIFE (JOHN 3:16). WHAT AN EXAMPLE TO FOLLOW! LEARNING TO LOVE MORE LIKE GOD IS ONE OF THE BIGGEST CHALLENGES OF RELATING TO PEOPLE THE WAY GOD INTENDS. RELATIONSHIPS ARE MEANT TO BE DEEP, LASTING, AND LIFE CHANGING. TOO MANY PEOPLE TREAT RELATIONSHIPS LIKE A NEW CAR WITH ALL THE BEST OPTIONS. THEY LIKE IT WHEN THEY BUY IT, BUT BEFORE TOO LONG SOMETHING NEW COMES OUT—SO THEY TRADE IN THEIR OLD CAR FOR THE LATEST MODEL. GOD DID NOT CREATE THROWAWAY PEOPLE. NEITHER DID HE CREATE US TO BE INVOLVED IN THROWAWAY RELATIONSHIPS. HE DID CREATE ALL OF US WITH THE NEED TO LOVE AND BE LOVED. "WE LOVE EACH OTHER BECAUSE HE LOVED US FIRST" (1 JOHN 4:19). THE BETTER WE BECOME AT LIVING IN A PROPER RELATIONSHIP WITH GOD, THE BETTER WE WILL BE AT UNDERSTANDING AND MAINTAINING HEALTHY RELATIONSHIPS WITH THOSE AROUND US. SO LET'S GET ON WITH IT!

NSHIPS ♥

MOVING BACK HOME
AFTER COLLEGE | A FIELD GUIDE

2414

You CHOSE A COLLEGE, A MAJOR, AND A CAREER hoping that graduation would lead to a job netting forty grand a year with benefits and preferred parking. Instead, your alarm goes off beside the bed you slept in during high school, your forty-grand position is an entry-level job changing oil at the Fast Lube, your benefits are room and board that are worse than the college dorm, and your preferred parking is anywhere but in front of the mailbox.

They should have told you what your college degree would get you. An athletic major gets you a job at Foot Locker. A degree in literature wins you a slot at Barnes & Noble. A communications major means you're the trainer for drive-thru headset etiquette. If you find yourself in a situation like any of these, here are some things to keep in mind when you move back in with Mom and Pop:

IT ALL DEPENDS ON HOW YOU LEFT

If you left on good terms, the road back home should be smooth. Still, it's important to be totally honest and open with your parents. Don't just show up and assume that it's okay to put your underwear back in the drawers. And if your parting words were, "Hey, I'm an adult now, you can't tell me what to do. I'm outta here!" . . . well, the road may be a little tougher. Don't be surprised to step onto the front porch and hear your dad say, "I'd offer you something to eat, but it looks like you're choking on your pride." Now's your chance to let your parents know that you're going to do everything you possibly can to turn your life around.

BE PREPARED TO PAY TO STAY

You no longer get to sit on the couch eating cheese doodles while watching

SportsCenter or *Trading Spaces*. The only time you get to do that is when your shift ends at your second job. Your presence increases household expenses. Your parents shouldn't have to dig into their savings to cover your costs. Maybe you're not ready to make it on your own, but at least carry your own weight as much as you can until you are. Be ready to pay rent, share expenses, or take on daily household responsibilities.

BEHAVE YOURSELF

Clear communication is more important than ever. Make certain you understand your parents' expectations. Never forget: You've moved back in as a guest—you need to live like one. Show respect and you'll get respect in return. It may not be easy to abide by the house rules after you've been out on your own, but do it anyway. Wash your own dishes and clothes, buy some groceries without being asked, and don't violate the fire marshal capacity of your room's maximum occupancy.

Many twentys choose to move back in with their parents these days. If you make that choice, don't throw your hands up in defeat. This isn't a defeat—it's a great opportunity for you to save money and prepare for the road ahead. And your parents will likely be fine with the arrangement as long as you freely remind them that you know your place, and ultimately it's on your own. • • • • • • • • • • • •

PARENTS REALLY CAN BECOME
• FRIENDS

Your relationship with your parents has been changing since the time you were born, whether you realize it or not. Your level of dependence (hopefully) has been steadily decreasing as you've gotten older. Think about it for a moment. As a baby, you were far more dependent on your parents than you were as a five-year-old. By the time you hit your teen years, you were reaching new levels of independence, and this continued as you moved out of the house for college or life on your own. This trend is likely to continue until the pendulum swings and your parents become increasingly dependent on you. But odds are, you're not there yet.

While the process begins in your late teens, it's primarily during your twentys that parents begin transitioning into being friends. That doesn't mean they're no longer your mom and dad—they'll likely be a much-needed resource for advice, wisdom, support, encouragement, and quick emergency loans for years to come. But the time has come for them to trust you as a fellow adult. This is easier for some parents than others. If your parents have a hard time seeing you as an adult and still want to dress you in OshKosh B'Gosh, then you may need to sit down and have a talk with them. Give them examples of how you're taking responsibility for yourself, and ask them to consider redefining the relationship. Let them know you want to have a stronger friendship with them. While it may require time and effort, the change will ultimately lead to a closer relationship overall.

You may not realize it, but many parents of twentys are looking for approval and positive feedback. They need to hear from you that you appreciate the way they raised you and the job they did as parents. Even if you had some rough years growing up, find some positive things to say or wonderful memories to highlight. Recognize the sacrifices they made to bring you where you are today.

Then begin acting like a friend. Take your parents out for a meal and insist on paying. Spend a day shopping, playing golf, or doing activities that you enjoy together. And verbally praise your mom and dad as they transition into the friendship stage of the parenting relationship. • • • • • • • • • • • • • • • • • • •

PERSONAL COMMUNITY
(PUR-SUN-AL CUM-YOO-NIH-TEE):
The lump sum of relationships in your life.

Your posse. Your tribe. Your people. Call it what you may—you were designed for a personal community. You were meant to have healthy relationships that challenge you, empower you, and encourage you to live your best life.

A healthy personal community is like a spiderweb that connects all the relationships in your life including your friends, family, mentors, coworkers, and others. If you intentionally develop a strong, well-rounded personal community, you will have a foundation to help you celebrate life's triumphs and weather life's storms. As you reflect on your personal community, think about the following:

FRIENDS

Friendship is one of the cornerstones of any healthy personal community, and twentys place a tremendous value on friendship. In fact, for many of you who live far from home, friends have become a substitute for family. Think Ross, Joey, Monica, Phoebe, Chandler, and Rachel! When birthdays or job promotions come along, you celebrate with friends who are nearby rather than family members who are far away. If you want to build a healthy personal community, pick friends who support and challenge you and don't tear you down or ask you to compromise your beliefs. When you find good friends, you're finding a good future.

FAMILY

Even if Rand McNally or MapQuest tells you your family is 1,046.7 miles away, relatives are still an integral part of your personal community. No matter what the distance, your family gives you roots and context for life. They remind you where you've been and hopefully help chart a healthy course for where you're going. During your twenties, your family may grow as siblings marry and nieces and nephews are born. Your relationship with your parents will change, too, and you may find yourself taking care of others rather than being taken care of. Now that you're a full-on adult, your family relationships can develop in ways you never could've experienced before.

MENTORS

You don't have to apply for a slot on *The Apprentice* to find someone who knows more than you do about business or life. Most likely, there's already someone in your community right now just waiting to offer you wise counsel. If you don't already have a mentor or someone older you can call on for wisdom or guidance, then it's time to start seeking out this type of relationship. Mentors are a rich addition to your personal community. A good mentor offers guidance, support, and wisdom. Look around—whether you find a mentor at church or at work, you will benefit greatly from the insight just waiting to be gained through that relationship.

FAITH COMMUNITY

You are not an island. God wants you to enjoy the richness of a community of believers. You were designed to fellowship with people who share your faith and can hold you accountable and help you grow. As you pray and worship together, you'll be strengthened in your spiritual journey. This is your opportunity to bless others and to be blessed too!

It takes work to develop a healthy personal community, but it's well worth the effort! These relationships will set you on the path to a fulfilled and balanced life.

THE FIVE LEVELS OF FRIENDSHIP

ALL OF US NEED FRIENDS. When we were younger, it was easy to pick our friends—we'd latch on to whoever said hi to us first. Those were the days when we could pass out valentines to the whole class without being considered weird. But it got a little harder as we got older. The barometer soon changed from "Who said hi first?" to "Who accepted me for who I am?"

Our need for relationships is fierce. Research shows that friends make us healthier—unless we're sharing a glass at the height of flu season. Friends accept us, instill confidence, and give us courage to do things we wouldn't ordinarily do—like try out for the team, ask someone out on a date, or drink a six-pack of Scope.

In this high-tech age when so many people are floating alone in cyberspace, we need to remember that friendships are both important and necessary. There is no substitute for connectedness.

Do you long for meaningful relationships but wonder how to go about finding or developing them? Do you sense that there's a higher dimension to friendship that could make you happier, but you don't know how to find it? There are five basic levels of friendship, and knowing what those are can help you as you seek that sense of connectedness you long for:

PEOPLE YOU MEET

These are the people you happen to run into at the mall or when you're out with other friends. They have very little influence on your life because you may or may not ever see them again. But be aware that this group could very well contain someone who turns out to be extremely beneficial to your life.

PEOPLE YOU KNOW

You've interacted with these people before, and at least 80 percent of the time you call them by name when you see them out somewhere. You tend to watch what you say and do around these people because you'll probably see them again . . . and you're not quite sure who they know that you know. Look for common ground or something else that a more substantial relationship could be built on.

PEOPLE YOU HANG WITH

You depend on these friends to fill your empty time. They accept you for who you are, and you do the same for them. Be transparent with these people, and give them permission to tell you exactly how they see you both at your best and your worst.

PEOPLE YOU TRUST

These are the friends who tell you their secrets. But more important, you tell them your secrets. These are the relationships that have the greatest potential for hurt when the trust is violated—and the greatest potential for joy when the trust remains strong.

PEOPLE YOU WOULD DIE FOR

You know you can depend on these friends to be there for you no matter what. There's nothing you could do that would make them stop believing in you. Make certain you return the commitment. Go the extra mile in believing what they say. Refuse to make quick, unfounded emotional judgments. And above all, keep private the things they tell you in confidence.

Our hearts have room for only so many people. And the friends who are closest to our hearts will have the greatest impact on our lives. That's why we have to exercise caution when it comes to choosing the people we trust and the people we would die for. And if you choose wisely, you'll be rewarded with friends who not only love you but whose love will last a lifetime.

THE GREAT
ROOMMATE DEBATE

THEY SAY THAT LIVING WITH ROOMMATES is good training for life. It's the lab experiment for useful skills like compromise, communication, and conflict resolution. Oh, and let's not forget the all-important lessons on how to hang toilet paper on the dispenser properly and how to share—or not share—our most precious possessions. (Mi casa es su casa, but mi Dr. Pepper es *mi* Dr. Pepper!)

It also serves as valuable on-the-job professional training: Phone-message-taking skills can never be underestimated. And the lessons about dirty socks, openness and honesty, division of chores, and the importance of late-night ponderings offer a great practice field for marriage, too.

But living with roommates is not the best choice for everyone. When it's good, it's very good, but when it's bad, it's very bad. So when deciding what your next living arrangements will be, make sure you weigh out the pros and cons of all the options.

HAVING ROOMMATES—PROS:

MONEY Not only is the rent shared, but the utilities, cable, and Internet bills are, too. Most likely, a roommate will have appliances, furniture, or other furnishings to contribute as well. And buying consumables in bulk and sharing them can save more than you might think.

COMMUNITY Ideally, roommates are also friends who care about each other's lives. Having someone around to share your experiences can make life so much more bearable. And being available to listen to what they're going through is a great way to move beyond yourself and practice focusing on others. Besides all that, though, having roommates can add spice to life. Whether pummeling each other with pillows or playing Xbox or cooking dinner, life is just more fun when it's shared.

SUPPORT Weekends are so much happier when you're not the only one carrying the burden of household chores. And roommates are often available for airport runs and rides from the auto repair shop or doctor's office.

HAVING ROOMMATES—CONS:

PRIVACY Even when you have separate rooms, TVs, and phone lines, it's hard to keep from knowing everyone's business when you live together. That's just one of the realities of living in close proximity. There's no hiding who's coming and going or when.

PREFERENCES Everyone has his own opinion of how loud is too loud when it comes to music or TV. You probably also have different ideas about cleanliness and how often to entertain guests or host parties. Compromise must be reached about everything from noise control to what temperature the thermostat should be set on to how long dirty dishes should remain in the sink, and the list goes on.

CHANGE It is harder to get out of a lease or just pack up and move if you have a roommate who is depending on you. Things can also get complicated when you take a new job or need to make adjustments in your budget. Settling bills, handling the deposit, and separating belongings can cause trouble when it's time to move on.

All of the pros can be maximized and the cons minimized by simply choosing roommates wisely. But of course there's always some degree of conflict when dealing with another human being. It's a shame none of us are perfect, but how boring would that be anyway!

When deciding on a roommate, you may want to find someone who shares your preferences. If you like to sleep in, don't pair up with a loud early riser. If you are warm-blooded, don't choose someone who is cold all the time. In other words, find someone as much like you as possible. But no matter whom you choose to live with, there will always be issues that require you to compromise.

On the other hand, there may be some things that are nonnegotiable for your home. If you are allergic to cats, you probably shouldn't room with anyone who can't leave their furry critters behind. Or if you're allergic to mold, you might want to avoid roommates who like to leave their leftover tuna in the fridge for months at a time. Or if you can't deal with someone who is messy, you may need to either live alone or find a fellow neatnik.

The key is finding (and being!) someone who can contribute to a meaningful existence in a peaceful, healthy, fun dwelling place. Here are a few characteristics to look for when choosing roommates:

QUALITIES OF A GOOD ROOMMATE:

DEPENDABLE Even if they are just like you in every way and you've been very best friends since kindergarten, remember that you'll be signing a legally binding contract or lease together. Make sure they are financially stable enough to help pay the bills and dependable enough to trust with your good name and credit rating.

WILLING TO COMPROMISE You don't have to agree on everything as long as you are all willing to work together for a common solution. Talk about potential problems or differences up front. Watch for defensiveness or selfish traits as you discuss the idea and make plans for moving in together.

CONSIDERATE Watch how your prospective roommates treat or talk about others. Things you consider common courtesy might be completely foreign to them. Don't expect a sudden jump in consideration or kindness just because you become roommates! What you see now is what you'll get later.

YOUR ROLE AS A GOOD ROOMMATE:

PULL YOUR WEIGHT Be responsible by paying your part of the bills on time every month. Try not to make a habit of mooching off everyone else, and for goodness' sake, clean up after yourself! Your mama didn't move with you, so now it's all up to you! Pitch in with chores and let others know when and why you will be late in performing any agreed-upon task.

DEFINE & DECLARE EXPECTATIONS Your household will run much more smoothly if you proactively define roles, responsibilities, and ground rules from the beginning. You may get a little grief at first, but everyone will be glad you did it in the end. That's a guarantee!

COMMUNICATE As with any relationship, listening is key. Try to hear and understand your roommate's perspective. Be open and honest and confront situations or differences as they arise. One of the biggest misery makers is when feelings or concerns are bottled up inside and not expressed. Before long, you'll find yourself in that place where every single thing the other person does is annoying. Don't let it get that far!

5 DOs & DON'Ts
OF GOOD FRIENDS

Aristotle once said, "Without friends no one would choose to live, though he had all other goods." Having things is good; keeping friends is better. When we find a good friend, we need to do everything we can to keep the relationship strong. Here are some hints:

❶ Friends initiate—they don't invade. It's less about me and more about you.

❷ Friends question—they don't accuse. Friends think the best of each other and don't draw conclusions until they've gathered all the facts.

❸ Friends tell the truth—they don't deny it. We need to tell the truth in the right way at the right time—even when it's hard. Denying the truth denies the friendship.

❹ Friends respond—they don't run away. "Tell me how I can help." "No matter what, I'm here for you."

❺ Friends protect—they don't expose. Protecting our friends can cost us dearly. But exposing them will very likely cost us the friendship.

"A friend is always loyal, and a brother is born to help in time of need" (Proverbs 17:17).

By following these simple principles in your relationships, you can help take your friendships to the next level!

DIFFICULT PEOPLE DON'T HAVE TO GET THE BEST OF YOU

IF YOU THINK YOU CAN AVOID DIFFICULT PEOPLE by quitting your job, changing schools, or skipping the family holidays, think again. Difficult people are everywhere—from the checkout line at your local convenience store to the pew behind you in church. And if you don't watch out, they can get the best of you. So what are the best ways to handle difficult people?

REMEMBER THAT DIFFICULT PEOPLE ARE OFTEN JUST LOOKING FOR ACCEPTANCE. Many of them have been rejected so many times that they actually expect it. Whether they've read about the love and acceptance of Christ or not, they probably haven't experienced it. They're hungry to be accepted, encouraged, and loved—just as they are.

TRY TO LEARN MORE ABOUT THEIR BACKGROUND AND HISTORY. You may be struggling to understand why a person behaves or reacts a certain way, but the reasons may stem from an abusive or difficult past. Be sensitive, and try to learn more about the person—you'll be surprised by how compassionate you can be.

REMEMBER THAT EVERY PERSON IS VALUABLE TO GOD. It's not your place to critique a person's value—even when they do things differently. Sometimes God places difficult people in your life not so that they will change, but so that you will.

AVOID ASKING DIFFICULT PEOPLE TO GIVE WHAT THEY DO NOT HAVE. It's easy to fall into the trap of expecting people to change. But keep in mind that your way is not the only way. And maybe the person you're struggling with just can't live up to your expectations.

ASK GOD TO GIVE YOU EYES TO SEE PEOPLE AS HE SEES THEM. God is more than willing to give you grace and patience—and a new perspective. The reserved, sarcastic, socially awkward person you tolerate may be the precious child God longs to redeem, comfort, and heal.

ENCOURAGE OTHERS TO ACT WITH GRACE TOO. When a difficult person is thrust into a social situation, things can get awkward fast—for everyone. Be the one who steps up and makes a difference. Your attitude will influence your friends in ways that might surprise you.

CONFLICT RESOLUTION

Conflict is as much a part of life as bad service at a fast-food restaurant. Some people love conflict so much they run toward it like opposing medieval armies meeting on the field of battle. Others hate it so much that they'll do almost anything to avoid it. Avoiding conflict in a relationship is like smelling a carton of spoiled, lumpy milk from the refrigerator and putting it back thinking, *Maybe it'll be better tomorrow.* If you avoid conflict, it's only going to get worse.

So how do you deal? The first step is to recognize how you typically respond to conflict. Do you become an aggressor? Do you prefer to retreat? Do you demand immediate resolution, or do you suppress your feelings like nothing really happened?

Then you need to figure out how the other person responds to conflict. You may both prefer to dive right in to a heated discussion or pretend like nothing happened, but the healthiest choice is probably somewhere in between. Give each other time and space—whether it's a few hours or a few days—to cool down, and then revisit the subject when you can talk about it without distractions or stress. Remember to use "I felt" statements rather than accusatory "you" statements when discussing the topic. And once you've talked it through, commit to laying down the offense and refusing to pick it back up. This may take some practice, but stick with it. Preserving the relationship is more important than winning the conflict.

Everyone is different, and unfortunately a universal formula for conflict resolution doesn't exist. Many conflicts are pretty petty and stem from basic pride, jealousy, selfishness, or the desire to be in control. If you see recurring patterns in your conflicts with people, take a look at what those patterns reveal about you or any unresolved issues in your relationships. If past experiences are impacting present conflicts, it may help to talk about that. Sometimes conflict can be averted simply by stepping forward and being open and vulnerable. Remember that every conflict provides an opportunity for both humility and growth.

RELATIONSHIPS CHARGE US UP OR DRAIN US DRY

There are really only two types of relationships: those that charge us up and those that drain us dry. If the person you're hanging out with always has to choose what you do, where you eat, what movie you see, what you talk about, and whom else you hang out with, you're probably feeling pretty brittle right now.

But don't despair! God's Word says "he delights in every detail of [our] lives" (Psalm 37:23). He sees what you're dealing with and knows how to help. Ask God for his insight into the situation. Ask him if you need an attitude adjustment or if there's something you're doing that's aggravating the situation. You could even ask him whether you should continue the friendship or not.

When you begin involving God in your relationships, there's no telling what can happen. The other person might change, or then again you might be the one to be transformed. Fixing people and relationships is God's job—let him do it. He can recharge and refill you in ways you couldn't even imagine.

5 WAYS TO MESS UP YOUR RELATIONSHIPS

Our best efforts at building relationships can actually mess up our chances before we even get started. If your goal is to avoid relationships or just destroy the ones you already have, well then, here are five tips to help you down the path of relationship destruction:

BECOME STINGY WITH YOUR LIFE. Develop a passion for complete control. Like the child who's abandoned by his friends when he won't share his toys, you'll soon find yourself all alone in a corner somewhere.

NEVER OPEN UP. Contrary to popular belief, this is not the best way to avoid pain in a relationship. If you're not honest about how you feel, the other person never gets to know the real you. But if your goal is to mess up the relationship, keep your opinions to yourself.

TALK ABOUT YOURSELF ALL THE TIME. Know someone like this? How do you feel about them? Want everyone else thinking those thoughts about you? Keep on talking.

ALWAYS HAVE SOMETHING NEGATIVE TO SAY. Many of us have dated someone like this. Notice that the emphasis is on the past tense . . . *dated*.

MAKE YOUR FRIENDS FEEL LIKE THEY'RE JUST A SMALL PART OF YOUR PLAN FOR WORLD DOMINATION. Friendship is meant to be a two-way deal. If you're focused only on what you can get out of the other person, you're well on your way to messing up the relationship.

If you're reading this by yourself and can't think of anyone this describes better than you, then you really are the king or queen of bad relationships. **Congratulations!**

Twentys move a lot—and it can be tough keeping up with friends who live all over the country. But it's not impossible. Here are some resources for keeping your friendships strong:

KEEPING YOUR FRIENDSHIP ALIVE

1 E-mail. It's cheap. It's even free (with the right server). And it's immediate.

2 Instant messaging. See No. 1.

3 Snail mail. Nothing says "I really care" like an old-fashioned, handwritten letter.

4 Postcards. This is an alternative to No. 3 when you're *really* short on time and cash.

5 Gag gifts. Start a tradition of exchanging inexpensive but outlandish gag gifts throughout the year. Everyone needs a Ralph Nader action figure after the latest election.

6 Phone. Invest in a pre-paid calling card from Sam's Club or Costco. For a mere three cents a minute you can afford to call almost anyone in the United States and talk for a really, *really* long time.

7 Road trips. Hop in the car with too much junk food and too little time and spend the weekend with those you love.

8 Organize an annual reunion. Find a cool city or sunbaked beach where all your friends from high school or college can meet, and spend a few days reconnecting.

JUICY GOSSIP OR GOOD
· · · · · · · · · · · · · · · CONVERSATION?

There's nothing quite like catching up with friends and getting the 4-1-1 on what's going on in everyone's life. But sometimes we cross the line from good conversation to juicy gossip. So what's the difference? It usually comes down to a question of motivation. The Bible reminds us that "people may be pure in their own eyes, but the Lord examines their motives" (Proverbs 16:2).

Here are some questions to consider when discerning whether or not you're caught up in gossip:

DO THE WORDS UPLIFT, ENCOURAGE, AND SUPPORT RECONCILIATION, OR DO THEY CAUSE DIVISION?

HAVE YOU SPOKEN TO THE PERSON DIRECTLY ABOUT THE INFORMATION YOU'RE SHARING?

DO YOU THINK YOU WOULD HAVE THE PERSON'S PERMISSION TO SHARE THE INFORMATION?

WOULD YOU FEEL COMFORTABLE SHARING THE INFORMATION IF THE PERSON WERE IN THE ROOM?

DO YOU FEEL ENCOURAGED AND CHALLENGED AFTER THE CONVERSATION, OR ARE YOU ASHAMED, BITTER, OR ANGRY?

By examining your own motives and the fruit of your words, you can get a good sense of when you've crossed the line. Some things are just better left unsaid. Proverbs 10:19 says, "Too much talk leads to sin. Be sensible and keep your mouth shut." In the end, everyone will benefit from your discretion.

WHAT DID YOU JUST SAY?
TIPS FOR BECOMING A BETTER LISTENER

Do you ever find your mind wandering when someone is talking? How often have you found yourself wondering, *What did he just say?* And have you ever endured the humiliating moment when the person doing the talking realizes that you haven't been listening? If so, you're not alone. Fortunately, you can become a better listener. Here's how:

REMOVE YOUR PERSONAL BIAS. This can be tough. Many of us have unspoken ideas and expectations that inhibit our ability to listen. Do your best to go into every conversation with a clean slate.

BEGIN TO RECOGNIZE NONVERBAL CUES. It's estimated that up to 65 percent of a person's meaning is expressed through nonverbal communication, including posture, gestures, and facial expressions. If you "listen" for nonverbal cues, you'll be surprised how much easier it is to understand what's truly being said.

REPEAT THE SPEAKER'S WORDS BACK TO HIM. Say something like, "What I hear you saying is . . ." This will clear up any misunderstandings and make sure you're on the same page.

REMOVE INTERRUPTIONS. Turn off your cell phone. Turn down the CD player. Shut the windows if it's noisy outside. Do what it takes to remove anything that might distract or interrupt the conversation.

BE HONEST. If all else fails, just be honest with the other person. Tell her that you're distracted or preoccupied. It's not much, but at least your honesty will be appreciated.

Kissing Friends

Ah, yes, the classic kissing friend. You get together with a hottie and smooch. No sex. No danger. And best of all: no commitment. It's just kissing, right? It's just kissing as long as it stays just kissing, but all too often relationships between kissing friends get complicated. You wouldn't be kissing unless you were attracted to each other at least a little, right? Issues are guaranteed to arise when one or the other kissing friend wants to take the relationship to the next level. Suddenly you're faced with the decision of compromising your purity by becoming sexually active or breaking the relationship off completely. Kissing friends may be fun, but there is a danger involved—like getting hurt or hurting someone else. That's why it's better to draw healthy boundaries in a relationship, like skipping the kissing until there's some form of commitment.

DATING FROM A to Z

Dating can be confusing. And sometimes it feels like we get it wrong all the way from A to Z. Here's how some of us might spell out the alphabet of our latest traumatic dating experience:

A ALONE the desperate kind

B BEGINNING

C CUTE

D DUMB matching sweaters

E EXPRESS commitment by leaving your stuff at each other's house

F FUNNY pet names

G GRINNING while saying nothing

H HYSTERICAL— everything that was once cute now gets on your nerves

I IT'S NOT YOU . . . well, actually it is

J J.B.F.—let's *just be friends*

K KEEP telling yourself it'll be okay—it's all you've got

L LET it go

M MOODY

N NEUROTIC

O OPEN-MINDED —which means lower your standards

P PANIC— again, the desperate kind

Q QUESTION: "It wasn't all that bad, was it?"

R RATIONALIZING

S SETTLING

T TELLING yourself that they weren't the creep your friends said they were

U UNEXPLAINABLE urge to leave

V VENDETTA— where you pray the trials of Job on your ex

W WAH! Why me?

X X—You either are one or you have one. Welcome back. We missed you while you were gone.

Y YELLING

Z ZERO—end game

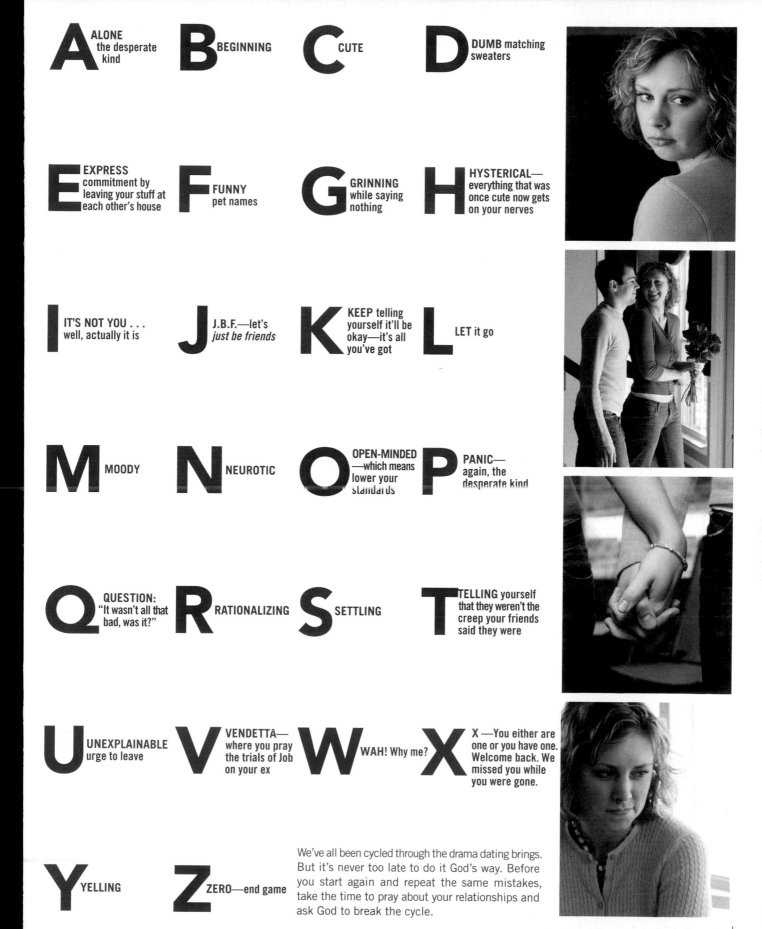

We've all been cycled through the drama dating brings. But it's never too late to do it God's way. Before you start again and repeat the same mistakes, take the time to pray about your relationships and ask God to break the cycle.

A NEW PERSPECTIVE ON PURITY

"Blessed are the pure in heart, for they shall see God" (Matthew 5:8, NASB).

The subject of purity shouldn't stimulate a panic attack. You don't have to live a boring life in order to be pure. In fact, purity is more about what we say yes to than about what we say no to. Here is a chart that should help:

WHAT PURITY ISN'T

AN ELABORATE SYSTEM OF DOS & DON'TS

DIVIDING LIFE INTO TWO COMPARTMENTS —THINGS THAT ARE RELIGIOUS AND THINGS THAT AREN'T

THINKING THAT *ANYTHING* HAVING TO DO WITH OUR SEXUALITY IS UNCLEAN

PERFECTIONISM

THE LOSS OF PERSONAL IDENTITY

THINKING THAT WE CAN MAKE OURSELVES PURE BY MAKING OURSELVES BETTER

WHAT PURITY IS

PAYING MORE ATTENTION TO THE CONDITION OF OUR HEARTS THAN TO THE CONDITION OF OUR BODIES

DOING THE BORING BUT NECESSARY THINGS WITH EXCELLENCE

TRANSPLANTING OUR SPIRITUAL LIVES INTO OUR ACTIVITIES AND ACTIONS

A PROCESS IN PROGRESS

FOCUSING ON THE DESIRES OF GOD

TEN GREAT FIRST DATES

❶ Drive-in theater. Fun, adventuresome, and you don't have to talk if you don't want to.

❷ Hip restaurant. You can always talk about the food and décor if you run out of topics.

❸ Downtown stroll. Whether you live in a city or a town, spend an afternoon together visiting those shops you haven't visited in a while.

❹ Rock concert. Who would turn down tickets to a great show?

❺ Amusement park. Anyone who can't have fun at an amusement park doesn't deserve a second date.

❻ Snowball fight. Get some friends together for an afternoon of snow wars! Just be sure to institute the "no ice-balls" rule so no one gets hurt.

❼ Picnic. Find a basket and put together an old-fashioned picnic in a park.

❽ Bowling. For lots of laughs, go to the local bowling alley for a game or two.

❾ Chefs for a day. Whether it's Mexican, Chinese, or American, spend an afternoon or evening cooking together.

❿ Exercise. Go for a hike. Go snowboarding. Walk around the lake. Get out there and enjoy the outdoors together.

DID YOU KNOW?

PLUGGING PORN AT WHAT COST?

It is estimated that 60% of all Web sites are pornographic in nature.
(Source: MountainStudents.com)

TOP TEN LIES CHRISTIANS USE

TO HIDE THE TRUTH ABOUT BREAKING UP

1. "It's not God's will."

2. "I need to date Jesus for a while."

3. "I think we should just be prayer partners."

4. "I can't date anyone who's never heard of Carman."

5. "The Lord told me . . ."

6. "Dating my brother/sister in Christ is too much like falling in love at a family reunion."

7. "My accountability group made me do it."

8. "You speak in tongues better than you kiss in tongues."

9. "You never ask God to bless the salad or the appetizers."

10. "God has promised me exceedingly, abundantly above all I could ever ask or imagine, and, well . . ."

RELATIONSHIPS QUOTES "

"Friendship is the source of the greatest pleasures, and without friends even the most agreeable pursuits become tedious."

—St. Thomas Aquinas

"The older you get, the fewer slumber parties there are, and I hate that. I liked slumber parties. What happened to them?"

—Drew Barrymore in a *Cosmo* interview

THE FIVE LEVELS OF FRIENDSHIP CAN ALSO BE SEEN IN THESE ANSWERS TO THE QUESTION, *"DO THESE JEANS MAKE MY BUTT LOOK BIG?"*

TRUE BLUE, LIKE JEANS

PEOPLE WE MEET—"No—in fact, they're baggy. You must spend two hours a day on the treadmill!"

PEOPLE WE KNOW "No, they look fine. And they'll probably stretch over time, so you could even wear a smaller size!"

PEOPLE WE HANG WITH—"Well, that pair does, but we just ate lunch so it's not a fair question."

PEOPLE WE TRUST—"Actually, that pair does, but try black jeans or a pair with vertical stripes."

PEOPLE WE WOULD DIE FOR—"Why are you trying on jeans when you should be on a treadmill?" •

A SINGLE'S SEARCH FOR CONTENTMENT

If you're a single in your twentys, the world is your oyster! It's a great time to be you! This is your opportunity to live out your own personal declaration of independence. But no doubt there are times when you struggle with the challenges of the single life. There are moments when your heart screams, *I'm so content!* as you enjoy the careless freedom of impromptu adventure. But there are other times when the silent apartment and empty microwave dinner box change your heart's cry to, *I'm so lonely!* Sometimes Jesus is more than enough, and other times you wonder where God really is in all this.

It's a total paradox. And it makes no sense whatsoever to those who do not walk in your shoes. But that dichotomy is exactly what makes this time in life such an adventure. As Dickens wrote, it is "the best of times" and "the worst of times" all at once. Thank goodness your level of contentment is not summed up by where you stand at any given moment.

And why is this quest for contentment so closely identified with singleness anyway? No marriage license, honeymoon, or perfect mate can give you the gift of contentment. If you're not content deep down inside right now, it's a deeper issue than what is or isn't on your left ring finger. True contentment can be found only in surrender to the Giver of every good and perfect gift!

What does contentment, this elusive thing everyone's talking about and searching for, look like? It looks like surrender. Not surrender as in hopelessly giving up, but surrender as in offering something up to God and letting go of it. The Bible says that "God will meet all your needs according to his glorious riches in Christ Jesus" (Philippians 4:19, NIV). Make the decision to trust him with your life.

RELATIONSHIPS QUOTES

"Don't be concerned for your own good but for the good of others."
—1 Corinthians 10:24

The joys and challenges of finding contentment as a single in your twentys are numerous. But make no mistake—"single" defines a marital status, not a person. And the contentment you seek truly can be found . . . when you surrender to your faithful, loving Savior.

TRUE LOVE PASSES EVERY TEST

People rely on the weirdest things as "signs" that they're meant to be in love:

"I met him in the reception line of my friend's wedding. That must be a sign."
"I drive past her house every day." (Never mind that you live two doors down.)
"He always comments on how nice my hair looks." (The fact that he's a stylist should't matter, should it?) *"We have so much in common. I mean, we both drink water!"*
"He looked right at me." (Maybe that spinach between your teeth had something to do with it?) *"Of all the apartments he could have broken into . . ."*

Here's the good news: There are better ways to find your soulmate. In 1 Corinthians 13, the Bible reveals five tests for discerning whether or not you've found true love:

1. "DOES THE RELATIONSHIP STAND THE TOUGH TIMES?" (v. 7 "bears all things, believes all things" NASB) The way you and your "significant other" handle conflict reveals a lot about your character. Do you yell and scream at each other? Does one of you withdraw at the first sign of disagreement? Do either of you stop to really listen? Do you seek first to understand before demanding to be understood?

2. "CAN I BE TOTALLY HONEST?" (v. 6 "rejoices with the truth" NASB) Do you have to compromise what you believe for the sake of the relationship? Do you find yourself downplaying the importance of your faith? Do you feel the freedom to say what you really think?

3. "CAN WE SPEND TIME TOGETHER WITHOUT TOUCHING?" (v. 5 "does not seek its own" NASB) If you build your relationship on sex and then get married, what happens when sex is no longer enough and other things become more important? What if you find yourselves buried in debt? It doesn't matter how great the sex is if marital intimacy is constantly interrupted by bill collectors' phone calls.

4. "DO I WORRY ABOUT WHO HE'S WITH WHEN HE'S NOT WITH ME?" (v. 4 "love . . . is not jealous" NASB) This is a clear sign that you've been hurt in another relationship and haven't healed yet. Talk about it with the one you love. And if that proves too difficult, it's probably a good time to look for counselors in the Yellow Pages.

5. "AM I WILLING TO WAIT EVEN THOUGH I WANT TO RUSH AHEAD?" (v. 4 "love is patient" NASB) "He is so good looking! If I miss this chance, it may never come my way again." "She has a great career! I may never meet someone like this again." Don't rush things out of fear or panic. Take it slow and trust God with your future.

God knows how tricky love can be, and he wants only the best for us. It pays to be discerning and follow his advice.

MARRIAGE CHANGES EVERYTHING

Marriage changes everything. You can see it in the eyes of newlyweds and oldlyweds. There's something magical, mysterious, and wonderful that happens when two people commit to being together through thick and thin for the long haul. They experience love, forgiveness, and personal growth on a whole new level. They learn how to embrace and be embraced despite faults and weaknesses. And they learn to celebrate the big and small joys of life.

When you get married, the days of *Bridget Jones's Diary* may be over, but a new life has begun—one in which you'll learn about the importance of communication and compromise. You'll discover things not just about your partner but also about yourself. And you'll find that changing some of your habits—like drinking out of the milk carton or leaving your dirty socks on the floor—can go a long way toward putting a smile on your spouse's face. And it's those little smiles that keep you engaged, challenged, and joyful beyond measure.

So maybe change isn't such a bad thing after all.

DID YOU KNOW?

SEXUAL REGRETS?

80% of three thousand women surveyed regretted having casual sex before marriage. *(Source: The Happy Hook-up: A Single Girl's Guide to Casual Sex, Ten Speed Press, 2004)*

THE JOYS (AND TRIALS) OF SEX

It's no secret that you should wait to have sex until you're married, but it's not just because the Bible tells you so (although that's a good reason!). The fact is that sex is something that's too wonderful, special, powerful, and vulnerable to experience with just anyone. When you have sex with someone, you're not just giving your body—you're giving a part of yourself that you can never take back. The love and fullness of sex was designed to be experienced within the confines of marriage as a source of pleasure and protection. When you have sex, you join yourself to another person—not just physically, but in a deeply spiritual, emotional, and mysterious way. It's a holy union.

Waiting until you've said "I do" isn't always easy. But you can make the choices necessary to stay sexually pure. And not only is it possible, but it's so worth it. Just ask anyone who has waited until their wedding night to cash in on the experience. No flashbacks. No bad memories. Just pure, unadulterated pleasure that increases with practice. Who knew? God wants married couples to experience the mysterious, wild gift of sex in all its fullness over a lifetime together. How could anyone ever grow bored?

6 Myths About Marriage

Too often marriages are built on myths.
Here are six popular marriage myths and the truths that set them straight:

MYTH: YOU'LL NEVER BE LONELY AFTER YOU'RE MARRIED.
TRUTH: *Marriage isn't a panacea to loneliness, but with a little effort from both sides, marriage can be more fulfilling and wonderful than you ever imagined.*

MYTH: IF YOU TRULY LOVE EACH OTHER, YOU WON'T HAVE ANY PROBLEMS.
Truth: *Marriages have problems now and then just like all relationships do. Do what you can to minimize the hard times by preparing for them ahead of time.*

MYTH: MARRIAGE MAKES A PERSON A COMPLETE HUMAN BEING.
TRUTH: *Only our relationship with Jesus Christ makes us truly complete.*

MYTH: EVERYONE SHOULD BE MARRIED.
TRUTH: *The marriage God wants most is the one we have with him through Christ.*

MYTH: MARRIAGE MAKES PEOPLE HAPPY.
TRUTH: *External circumstances don't provide lasting happiness. True happiness comes from being content in Christ.*

MYTH: FAMILY BACKGROUND HAS NO EFFECT ON MARRIAGE.
TRUTH: *We all bring past experiences into our relationships. If we are carrying the pain of past hurt, we need to turn to Christ for help and healing.*

"Marriage is to be held in honor" (HEBREWS 13:4, NASB).

WORK–AN INTRODUCTION

THINK BACK TO YOUR VERY FIRST JOB. MAYBE IT WAS MOWING YOUR NEXT-DOOR NEIGHBOR'S YARD, WALKING THE FAMILY'S PET DOBERMAN, OR BABYSITTING YOUR FAVORITE TWO-YEAR-OLD TWIN COUSINS. WHATEVER YOUR FIRST JOB MIGHT HAVE BEEN, IT WAS NO DOUBT A FAR CRY FROM THE WORK YOU'RE DOING TODAY. STARBUCKS BARISTA OR TECHNICAL ASSISTANT OR CUSTOMER SERVICE REPRESENTATIVE—THE WORKING WORLD OF A TWENTY-SOMETHING IS A LOT MORE COMPLEX THAN WHAT THAT COLLEGE TEXTBOOK (OR MOM AND DAD FOR THAT MATTER) SAID IT WOULD BE. WORK IS CERTAINLY AN INTERESTING PART OF LIFE. SOME OF US GO TO COLLEGE AND BECOME TRAINED AT A PARTICULAR SKILL OR PROFESSION. SOME EVEN GO ON TO GRAD SCHOOL, MED SCHOOL, OR LAW SCHOOL BEFORE ENTERING WHAT SOCIETY CONSIDERS THE MORE LUCRATIVE POSITIONS. OTHERS GRADUATE FROM HIGH SCHOOL AND IMMEDIATELY ENTER THE "REAL WORLD." REGARDLESS OF YOUR JOB TITLE, WORK IS STILL THAT THING THAT MONOPOLIZES A HECK OF A LOT OF YOUR TIME AND ENERGY. MOST PEOPLE SPEND MORE TIME AT THEIR JOBS THAN THEY DO AT HOME. IN FACT, IF YOU WORK EIGHT TO TEN HOURS A DAY FIVE DAYS A WEEK FOR FORTY-FIVE YEARS, YOU'LL HAVE SPENT CLOSE TO THIRTEEN YEARS OF YOUR LIFE WORKING. *THIRTEEN YEARS.* HOW ARE YOU GOING TO SPEND THOSE THIRTEEN YEARS? DO YOU HAVE THE TOOLS YOU NEED TO SUCCEED? CHANCES ARE, YOU HAVE A PRETTY GOOD UNDERSTANDING OF WHAT WORK REQUIRES–AFTER ALL, YOU DIDN'T SPEND ALL THOSE HOURS BEHIND A CURBSIDE LEMONADE STAND FOR NOTHING. JUST REMEMBER: WORK IS MORE THAN A JOB–IT'S PART OF THE DEFINITION OF *YOU.* WHETHER YOU ARE A TEACHER OR A CONSTRUCTION WORKER, BE HUMBLE, BE JOYFUL, AND BE WHO GOD CREATED YOU TO BE.

WORK

IN BOX

1 Your new coworkers don't see you as a senior or even a sophomore. You're just the new kid.

2 The friends you've had for the last four years are now living in five states.

8

AWFUL REALIZATIONS

AFTER GRADUATION

3 Your boss expects you to work all day *every* day, even during the summer.

4 It's time to lose the freshman fifteen.

5 Brownnosing at work stinks.

6 They weren't kidding about student loans—six months after graduation the bills start rolling in.

7 The landlord doesn't take an IOU, spare change, or canned food in exchange for rent.

8 A hard-earned degree and a dollar still won't buy you a cup of coffee at Starbucks.

Write a MISSION STATEMENT

DO YOU KNOW WHERE YOU WANT TO GO IN LIFE? Well, here's some hard news for you: People who don't have a plan of action usually don't end up getting where they want to go. Surprisingly, most people don't fail because they lack knowledge or willpower or guts—they fail because they don't have direction. They need a career roadmap. Creating a personal mission statement will give you a clear sense of purpose and a basis for defining all of your activities, who you are, and what you're about.

Remember 1996's *Jerry Maguire*? Jerry, the type A character played notoriously by Tom Cruise, is struggling with his purpose, direction, and personal values. Driven by frustration and failure, he decides to write down a mission statement—"a suggestion for the future of our company," as he calls it. Jerry lists the "simple pleasures," "protecting clients in health and injury," "caring," and "being the me I always wanted to be" among his personal and professional values. That doesn't sound too hard, does it?

Writing your own mission statement will help you establish what's important to you before you even start your career. But that's not all. A personal mission statement will equip you to chart a new course when you're at a career crossroads.

There are plenty of resources available to help you with all of this. Life cheerleader and career advisor extraordinaire Stephen Covey wrote a great book titled *First Things First*, which asks the question, "Why worry about saving minutes when you might be wasting years?" Ouch! Wouldn't you like to know where you're going and how to get there instead of wandering around aimlessly for years on end? Another great resource that will help you get started is Laurie Beth Jones's book *The Path: Creating Your Mission Statement for Work and for Life.*

But don't complicate it. Spend an hour or two at your favorite coffee shop and begin writing down your thoughts on life—your ideals, values, what makes you tick. You may find that it doesn't take long to get a pretty clear idea of where you want to go in life.

And remember: Your mission statement might change a little as you get older—but that's okay! Just get one written down sooner rather than later because you don't want to wake up one day when half your life is over and wonder where in the world you are.

Four Questions to Ask Yourself: 1. What are my core values? 2. What motivates me to be my best? 3. What do I want to be doing three, seven, and fifteen years from now? 4. What do I have to offer an everyday work environment?

FIND A MENTOR; BE A MENTOR

(AN EXCHANGE BETWEEN TWO TWENTYS)

From: GBlovesGirls@uno.com
Dear Mr. Dustin McRoberts, this is Gary Beauchamp. You might remember me from Hillside Church's youth group. I'm now a 20-year-old sophomore, studying business. One of my assignments is to find a mentor who is doing what I want to do and ask for career advice. I thought of you. Since I think you're successful, I was wondering if you might be interested in giving me some advice.
Let me know, GB.

From: MarriedMan1977@yippee.com
Yo Gary, good to hear from you. Of course I remember you. You're the big blond-headed guy with the goofy grin, right? I can't believe you're in college now. Dude, I'd be honored to share any advice I can. Let me know what you need and I'll do my best. BTW: Call me Dustin. I'm only 28, bro. :-) D.

From: GBlovesGirls@uno.com
Hi, Dustin. Goofy grin? Yeah, that's me. Thanks for helping me out. Here are my first questions: When you were my age, what did you want to do? Are you doing now what you wanted to do then? What advice do you have for someone like me who wants to launch a business career?

From: MarriedMan1977@yippee.com
Good questions, Gary. I had no idea what career I wanted when I was in college. My only goal was to *not* be a waiter when I turned 30. So I looked for any business opportunity I could find. I had several internships. I found out what I liked and what I disliked. And then I pursued what I liked. That help?

From: GBlovesGirls@uno.com
Yeah, thanks. So it's okay for me to not know exactly what I want to do?

From: MarriedMan1977@yippee.com
Dude, you're going to change your mind ten times. Of course it's okay to not have it all together at your age. I certainly didn't. And no, I'm not doing what I originally wanted to do.

From: GBlovesGirls@uno.com
You think we can get together for coffee? I would love to talk to you more about how you got where you are at such a young age. Next Tuesday work for you?

From: MarriedMan1977@yippee.com
Tuesday works for me. How about 12:30 at the Starbucks in the Village? I look forward to catching up with you. And hey—bring your resume. Who knows? Maybe I'll be able to find an opening for you in my company!

KEYS TO LEARNING ALL YOU CAN
FROM AN INTERNSHIP

KNOW THE CODE If the company you're working for has a policy manual, take some time to read it. Study the fine print. Brush up on the sections on benefits, dress code, and personal relationships. If everyone else is sporting a tie or pantyhose, you need to skip the casual attire. If it's more relaxed, try not to outshine your boss. Find someone trustworthy and ask if there's anything else you should know about what's expected of you.

NETWORK LIKE CRAZY

This is your big chance to make friends and influence people. Use the opportunity to meet as many people as possible. Look for ways to put your best foot forward professionally. Engage people in conversations. Collect business cards. Offer your own if you have one. You may find that one of the people you meet today can help you land a job, even years later on down the road.

ASK QUESTIONS

As an intern, you are in a prime position to ask as many questions as you can. Everyone knows you are there to learn, so ask away! Remember, though, that it's very important to ask with a humble attitude and a tone of voice that communicates curiosity, wonder, and a genuine desire to learn. Keep an eye on the nonverbal responses to your questions and back off if you sense impatience, frustration, or annoyance in the person you're asking.

DON'T GET DISCOURAGED

Internships aren't always fun. You're probably going to be asked to make more than one trip to the copy machine. Maintain a good attitude. Look for ways to go above and beyond in your job duties. And remain positive until the end. Remember, this job isn't forever. It's just a launching point to something bigger and better . . . like a steady paycheck!

WORK QUOTES ""

"When Sunday loses its fundamental meaning and becomes subordinate to a secular concept of 'weekend' dominated by such things as entertainment and sport, people stay locked within a horizon so narrow that they can no longer see the heavens."

—Pope John Paul II

6 INTERNSHIP DON'TS

① DON'T BE A KNOW-IT-ALL.
You don't know it all. Even if you think you do—you don't. We promise.

② DON'T BE AFRAID TO ASK QUESTIONS.
Remember, you're there to learn, not just to provide the company with free or cheap labor. They have a responsibility to teach you something about the real world. Don't leave empty-handed.

③ DON'T BAD-MOUTH THE COMPANY YOU'RE INTERNING FOR. Your internship may be hell on earth. A lot of them are. But remember, you never know who will end up hearing what you say—and you can't afford to burn bridges.

④ DON'T UNDERESTIMATE YOUR INTERNSHIP.
Even if you're stuck in the basement stuffing file folders in alphabetical order, your low-man superior might end up being the head of a powerful firm—you just never know.

⑤ DON'T SIMPLY EARN YOUR CREDIT.
Think of your internship as a stepping stone to the rest of your life. How well you work now will impact your ability to do something brilliant in the future. So do your best!

⑥ DON'T LEAVE WITHOUT SAYING THANK YOU.
Regardless of how much you loved or despised your internship, *always* write the HR department or your boss a thank-you letter for allowing you the opportunity to work with them. When they need to hire someone in the future, they're apt to remember the person who took the time to say thank you.

CONFESSIONS from an INTERVIEWEE'S
Nervous mind

You finally scored an interview. You'd kill to have the job. And you're even wearing a suit. You know you look good. God has heard your prayers. You're pumped. You're ready. You walk into the interviewer's office and brace yourself for the onslaught of questions.   ***What's your name?*** Sweet! An easy one!

Where did you hear about us? No-brainer.

Why do you want to work here? Well, um, there's parental pressure to get a job, the need to pay off student loans, the big trip to . . . Oh no, you're pausing! Just at the last possible non-awkward second, you regain control. You want to work here because you've heard great things about the company and this is in line with the career you've always wanted.

What do you offer that other candidates don't? Uh-oh. The questions are getting tougher. You're cuter, smarter, and gosh-darn-it, people like you. Wait, you can't give that answer—you'll bomb. You're a recent graduate, with little to no experience feeling completely over your head? Nope, that won't work either. And you used up your free stalling minutes on the last question. Rather than answer the question directly, you deflect and answer with another question: What kind of candidate are you looking for? Whew! You out-thought that one. Now you can use the interviewer's response to hand deliver the right answer. Smooth!

What are your biggest strengths and weaknesses? Strengths—that's easy: you're an energetic hard worker. Weaknesses—well, that seems a little personal, doesn't it? You're not about to have open confession here. In desperation, you refer to your mental list of strengths and decide to use one as a potential weakness. You "work too much" or "expect too much of yourself."

Where do you see yourself in five years?
Your knee-jerk response: "In this office with your job or your boss's job." You know that's the wrong answer, but if the shoe fits . . . Hmm. Quick, what's the answer? Rather than name a title like manager or coordinator that may or may not exist in the company, you opt for a more vague response. You hope your hard work and skill will be recognized and eventually you'll be promoted to a managerial-type position.

What kind of salary are you expecting?
Six, no—seven digits at least. And perks. Yes, lots of perks, including a car, a house, all bills paid for, and at least six weeks of vacation. Wait—this is an entry-level job. You quickly avoid giving an actual number by replying that you're open to whatever they consider an appropriate amount.

Any last questions?
You can think of only one: "Do I have the job or not?" But instead you ask about the overall strengths of the company, health-insurance coverage, and corporate culture. You smile, shake the interviewer's hand, and run to Target to buy some thank-you notes. You pop one in the mail to the interviewer before the day is over and go home to await the big news: **YOU GOT THE JOB!**

six steps to a successful INTERVIEW

1. STUDY YOUR RÉSUMÉ Make sure you can explain every point on your resume (especially if someone else helped you put it together!). Go through it ahead of time and practice talking about your qualifications and what you learned from each job or activity you included.

2. DO YOUR HOMEWORK Every company on earth has a Web site. Use it. (And if the company doesn't have a Web site, why in the world are you interviewing for a job *there* anyway??) Be sure you find out everything you can about what the company does and what it offers its employees. Google the company name and see if there has been any recent press about it. Check out its most recent quarterly earnings or annual report. Find a way to work your astute observations about corporate culture into the conversation during your interview.

3. PREPARE FOR THE NORM Nearly every unimaginative interviewer will ask you about your strengths and weaknesses. Don't be caught off guard. Have positive, honest answers ready to go. You should also be ready to explain what you would bring to the team, your goals for work and life, and why you are interested in this position at this company.

4. LOOK 'EM IN THE EYE Direct eye contact, even on a hard question, signifies that you are confident, competent, poised, and good under pressure. Eyes that dart about can communicate uncertainty, dishonesty, and even disinterest.

5. SPEAK TO THEIR DESIRES Re-read the job description and any other information you have about what the company is looking for. Memorize key words and find a way to smoothly work them into your answers during the interview. After all, you are exactly what they need, right? Make sure they know it! . . . But be smooth and natural about it, for heaven's sake!

\\\\\\\\\\\\\\\\ STUDY YOUR RESUME

6. DRESS TO THE HILT
This may sound obvious, but you'd be surprised. Some say they don't want to look like they're "trying too hard" or they "don't like to dress up." Well . . . tough! Remember, it is always better to be overdressed than to look like you aren't serious about the job.

IT'S ALL
NEGOTIABLE

WOULD YOU EVER STEP ONTO A CAR LOT and pay full price for that Hummer you've been eyeing? It's not likely. Why? Because everyone knows that a car's price is negotiable. Yet countless twentys accept salary and benefits packages from employers without question because they don't realize that compensation is negotiable too.

Negotiating isn't easy. Some people hate it. But if you want to be fairly compensated, you're going to have to get over yourself and learn to negotiate. Here are a few areas to address:

SALARY

This is the most obvious area of negotiation. It's important to educate yourself about the average pay for someone of your qualifications and skills in a particular line of work. (Monster.com is a good place to start.) And don't forget to factor in cost of living. Once you're on the payroll, it's a general rule of thumb that you should ask for a 5 to 10 percent bump in pay for your work every year, realizing that that is the beginning of negotiations.

INCENTIVE PAY

Ask about bonuses, perks, and rewards for meeting certain goals and standards.

TRAINING

Ask about additional training opportunities. You may find that your company is willing to pay for classes to further your career and education.

PAID LEAVE

If your job requires frequent travel, ask about paid leave. Depending on how much traveling you're doing, you may qualify for a car allowance or flextime.

OFFICE LOCATION

Who says you have to have the cubicle? It doesn't hurt to ask for a nicer location, desk, or computer.

Now that you have some negotiation points in mind, here are some tips on how to be an effective negotiator:

DEVELOP A PLAN

Make a prioritized list of what's important to you. Before you go into a negotiating scenario, decide what you're willing to budge on or not. Look for ways to reach a win-win solution to each of your negotiation points.

STAY RELAXED

This isn't the time to get emotional or worked up. Make a list of your requests and stick to it. If one request is denied, move on to the next. Try to be assertive without becoming aggressive.

MAKE YOUR REQUESTS EMPLOYER-FRIENDLY

You're more likely to get what you want if you present your requests in a way that's sensitive to your potential employer's needs. For example, if you want additional vacation time, clarify that you'd be willing to take the time off during the company's slowest business season and that you wouldn't take it unless you were sure everything under your management was operating smoothly.

If at all possible, don't leave things open-ended.

Be very specific when you make a request. Instead of asking for a bigger salary, ask for a particular amount. If your employer can't give a definite answer, ask when he'll be able to provide one.

After you negotiate your concerns, pinch yourself, jump up and down, and text message all your friends with the good news about your super-savvy negotiating techniques!

\\\\\ AFTER YOU NEGOTIATE YOUR CONCERNS, PINCH YOURSELF, JUMP UP AND DOWN, AND TEXT MESSAGE ALL YOUR FRIENDS.

DID YOU KNOW?

THE VIEW'S BETTER UP HERE

A new study shows that your height is linked to your paycheck. Each inch of height adds about $789 a year.

TEAM BUILDING

In today's stressful workplace, taking time out of an already overextended day to play games or climb ropes courses is often impractical. Try these quicker, less-involved ideas for building team unity:

HAVE A SANDWICH SWAP. Bring your favorite sandwich to the cafeteria at the set time and do some trading.

GIVE A PLAYER AWARD. Put a note of encouragement or appreciation inside a trinket box. The recipient keeps the note and writes a new one before passing it to the next deserving player.

MAKE A STARBUCKS RUN! Instead of meeting in a boring conference room, meet together in the viby, comfy atmosphere of Starbucks and drink expensive coffee.

START AN OFFICE DEVO. What will people think when they hear that you're a Jesus freak? Set up a time to discuss spiritual matters with your colleagues and find out.

The point is to create a strong team without wasting a lot of time and money. Be the one to make the difference!

BE A TEAM PLAYER!

WORK TEAMS ARE A FACT OF LIFE THESE DAYS, and they're not going away anytime soon. They can make or break your job satisfaction level and can either max out or tone down your stress load.

BE A PLAYER *(BUT NOT LIKE COLIN FARRELL)*

Being a good team player will help you enjoy the daily grind and will lead to lasting results both at work and in your own personal development. The best assets you have as a player are loyalty and dedication. Never bad-mouth your teammates under any circumstances, and do whatever it takes to carry your part of the load.

Good team players are dependable, trustworthy, and consistent. Find ways to encourage your teammates and let them know you appreciate all they are doing for the success of your work project.

CLARIFY THE ROLES *(CUZ, WHAT GOOD IS A LEFT HAND WHEN THE RIGHT HAND DOESN'T KNOW WHAT IT'S DOING?)*

Effective teams have clearly defined roles for each member. It's a good idea to actually write out each member's roles and responsibilities so there is never any doubt about who does what when. Completing the task is job one, so be sure to stay focused on your specific duties while trusting others with theirs.

In addition to task-related roles, there will be personality roles within the team. If you are ordinarily outgoing and funny, you may tend to be the team's stress reliever. Or if you're quiet and reserved, you might be the calming voice in the midst of a turbulent flurry of activity. Pay attention to these unspoken roles. If there's already a dominant joke teller on the team, you may want to tone down that part of your personality. Or if everyone on the team is quiet and reserved, you may need to tap into your assertive side to keep the team from floundering.

OBEY THE RULES OF COMMUNICATION *(KIND OF LIKE THE MOVIE* RULES OF ENGAGEMENT, *BUT WITHOUT SAMUEL L. JACKSON)*

Remember what your mom said when you were in grade school? "God gave us two ears and one mouth for a reason!" Try to listen more than you talk, at least during the initial stage of team development. Listen to the meaning behind your teammates' words, and ask for clarification if you think you're missing something.

And when it's your turn to address the team, be sure you communicate clearly and accurately. Seek out feedback on your communication style, and ask follow-up questions to make sure people truly understand what you're trying to say. (This is especially important in e-mail conversations, where it's oh-so-easy to miscommunicate without even knowing it.)

HANDLE CONFLICT IN A HEALTHY WAY (WORKPLACE VIOLENCE IS NEVER THE RIGHT CHOICE—DUH!)

Don't gloss over unpleasant realities. Face them head-on with honesty and sensitivity. Mind your nonverbal cues as well. Watch your tone of voice, facial expression, and body language. Try to be warm and open in tone and posture, and avoid looking or sounding defensive. Address issues quickly to avoid further problems.

TECH-SAVVY GADGETS THAT MAKE LIFE SIMPLER

IPOD—You can carry every song you own in the palm of your hand. Is there anything cooler than that?

BLACKBERRY—Check your e-mail, surf the Web, take notes, answer your phone—all in one. These masterful little gadgets make life much simpler for the person with a life on the go!

ONSTAR—This is possibly one of the coolest technologies to hit the market in years. For emergencies, directions, or even if you locked your keys in the car—OnStar can help!

WIRELESS HEADSET—It can be a little pricey, but this wireless wonder will revolutionize your life! And it's great fun when people mistakenly think you're talking to them or yourself.

BOSE NOISE-CANCELLING HEADPHONES—Your own silent retreat from the loud, cruel world any time you so desire!

TIVO—VCRs are *so* 1990s. This modern marvel preserves must-see TV with precise clarity and incredible ease. Hey—anything that started as a brand and became a verb's gotta be cool!

\\\\\\\\\\\\\\\\\\\\\\\\\\\\ BEING A GOOD TEAM PLAYER WILL HELP YOU ENJOY THE DAILY GRIND

HEY BOSS—THAT'S YOU

CONGRATULATIONS! You've finally graduated from low man on the totem pole. You may not be running the company, but you're a member of management and you've actually got people working for *you* now! Before you start dancing around the office hollering, "Who's your daddy?" when no one is looking, here are a few tips to remember:

START OFF ON THE RIGHT FOOT. Your fellow employees have already sized up what type of boss you'll be. Surprise them by being better than they expect. Don't be stingy with compliments and encouragement—praise them for work well done. And be careful about introducing all the changes you've been dying to make. Take it slow—you don't want a bunch of freaked-out employees on your hands!

SHOOT STRAIGHT. In order to go from being a good boss to a great boss, you need to establish clear goals and guidelines for your employees so they know how to measure their job performance. Now's your chance to motivate your employees to see their jobs as more than just the daily grind.

BE A TEAM PLAYER. Odds are you beat out a few of your current employees for the position you now hold. You're going to have to re-win their trust and affirm them as individuals. Look for ways to motivate your staff to work as a team.

ACCEPT REALITY. As a boss, you're going to want to make everything better. The reality is, though, that some things just can't be changed. Don't be discouraged when you see that you can't solve everything in a day!

STICK TO THE BASICS. The basics of good management never change: Listen to your employees. Be kind. Be fair. Catch people doing something right. Avoid micromanagement. Set your staff members up for success. Remember the "little people" who make you shine.

BOSS

"YOU'VE FINALLY GRADUATED FROM LOW MAN ON THE TOTEM POLE. NOW YOU'RE THE BOSS. EVERYTHING YOU'VE WANTED TO CHANGE NOW RESTS IN YOUR HANDS."

Be Confident, Be Passionate, BE HUMBLE

One thing you quickly learn at your first "real" job in your twentys is that this is *not* college. Suddenly you are a little fish in a big pond—even if the pond has only eight other people swimming in it. Gone are the days of making the dean's list and having the right answers. Now, with every meeting and every task, you must show that you are qualified for this job because if you don't, your first step toward a career might be over.

Understanding some key job principles will enable you to easily get into your company's groove and remind your boss why he or she hired you. So tomorrow when you go to work, remember these few pieces of wisdom. Suddenly Manic Monday won't seem so bad.

❶ **LOVE YOUR JOB:** You may not want to be there any longer than you have to, but you're there now. Life is too short to not love what you do. Make the most of every day and pour some passion into your work.

❷ **BE PC:** Though political correctness has taken on a negative connotation in some circles, being PC in the workplace is generally positive. You can be true to what you believe while still maintaining respect for others and their views. Follow Jesus' advice: "Love your neighbor as yourself" (Matthew 22:39).

❸ **SHOW HUMILITY:** Even if you had a dozen internships in college, you still don't know everything. Be humble, and go to work intending to learn something new. With that attitude, it'll happen—every day.

❹ **KNOW YOUR PLACE:** It's better to remain quiet as you learn the inner workings of your office than to be boisterous and have an opinion about everything.

❺ **ASK QUESTIONS:** While it is good to take things in and know your place, it's equally important to ask questions. It's better to admit you don't know something than to pretend that you do. Your coworkers will appreciate your honesty.

❻ **DEVELOP GOOD RELATIONSHIPS:** Good relationships are vital to job success. Be respectful and have fun!

❼ **DON'T WORRY IF YOU MAKE MISTAKES:** You *will* make mistakes on the job. And when you do—own up to it! Your coworkers will respect you for being trustworthy and dependable even when you make an error.

❽ **BE LIKE JESUS:** It doesn't matter if you are working at a church or an accounting firm—your attitude should reflect the mighty God you serve. In all that you do, remember the fruit of the Spirit: "love, joy, peace, patience, kindness, goodness, faithfulness, gentleness, and self-control" (Galatians 5:22-23).

\\\\\\\\\\\\ **LOVE YOUR JOB**

DON'T ABUSE YOUR POWER!

It's great to see how fast, how soon you're moving up the ladder.
Everyone talks about your age and wonders if it matters
That someone twenty-four should have this kind of pull. . . .
You proudly shrug and say out loud, "I am powerful!"

Your mommy and your daddy are happy about the job.
You've got an office with a view and a big intern named Bob.
A laptop is provided to help you rule your throne.
You proudly shrug and say aloud, "Gosh, I feel at home."

You get your staff together to make your introduction.

You say how glad, how proud you are to have this new position.

"Now get to work! I need your best to someday make me shine."

You clap your hands and tell yourself, "Gosh, this job is fine."

You're loud and you're obnoxious, and you like your iron thumb.
When someone questions your authority, you maturely say, "You're dumb."
There's no doubting your ability; your bosses are quite proud.
But one of your employees says, "I just can't take your mouth."

You hire someone new to replace the angry one.
You're staying late and working hard, ensuring all gets done.
Intern Bob is running 'round and pulling out his hair.
You roll your eyes and say out loud, "Your contentment's not my care."

Deadlines lurk around the corner; upper management is calling:
"Why aren't you finished with this project, and why are numbers falling?"
You quickly blame the brand-new hire: "She's just not up to snuff."
Intern Bob goes running when you scream, "Enough's enough!"

You head out on a rampage. Who should you clobber first?
The new girl? The intern? The lazy guy? Who here did the worst?
Your vocal chords are booming, "Where is intern Bob?"
Someone yells, "He's over here—fearing for his job!"

At that moment, your boss's voice screams
your name out loud.

"Why is a manager under my watch so
childishly acting out?

"I honestly thought you fit the bill,
but now I'm not so sure.

"Your talent's good, but not good enough.
I'm sorry, but there's the door."

All those around begin to shout, "Yes, we shall be free!"
Intern Bob runs up to your boss and kisses him on the knee.
You try to explain, you try to plead, but sadly it's just too late.
You humbly shrug and say out loud, "I hate my powerless fate."

Now the moral of this rhyme is for all
of you who lead:

You're young and you're ambitious,
but don't forget to heed

The advice of those much wiser who'll
help you blossom like a flower—

You'll never get where you want to be
if you abuse your power.

THE COLLIDING SIDES OF LIFE

"REAL" YOU

?

"PROFESSIONAL" YOU

"REAL" YOU Plays Xbox on Tuesday night with your closest friends. Writes beautiful poetry to make your "significant other" swoon. Works out at the gym four nights a week so you can keep your six-pack. Dreams about meeting Mr./Ms. Right at your church's singles' night. Counts the days 'til the new Orlando Bloom or Reese Witherspoon movie is released. Dreams of making it big in Hollywood. Parties like a rock star on Friday night *(the good, clean kind of party, of course)*.

"PROFESSIONAL" YOU Skips lunch so you can meet with coworkers about a new project. Is the head writer of a million-dollar advertising campaign that makes the boss proud. Comes to work forty-five minutes early so you can keep your job. Says that Mr./Ms. Right would only get in the way of career success. Is counting the estimated value of your 401(k). Hopes to keep your job during next month's downsizing. Sleeps like a rock after a long, exhausting day.

5 WORK HABITS OF JESUS

❶ JESUS HAD A PERFECT WORK ETHIC. He probably never had to read *The 7 Habits of Highly Effective People.*

❷ JESUS HAD A TEAM. Team support is always a good thing. And Jesus pulled good teamwork out of the same kind of imperfect, know-it-all sinners you work with every day.

❸ JESUS WAS A PROBLEM SOLVER. He wasn't discouraged by obstacles. He just found ways to overcome them.

❹ JESUS WORKED FOR HIS FATHER. We may not be in the family business, but we should work for our heavenly Father too!

❺ JESUS DEVELOPED A FOLLOWING *without* an online ad campaign, a publicist, a product, or Donald Trump.

It's not about being two-faced or hypocritical, it's just a fact of life: You're not the same at work as when you're hanging out with friends. You simply can't act like the goofball you really are when you're being a professional! Relax, though. It's okay and natural at this stage of life!

WORK VS. LIFE

DON'T LOSE THIS BATTLE!

You're in the groove. Getting tons of work done. Marking things off the endless to-do list. Suddenly your cell phone starts vibrating in your pocket. Hating to tear your eyes away from the mesmerizing facts and figures on the computer screen, you blindly retrieve the shaking little intruder and squeak out your greeting. The perturbed voice on the other end wakes you from your over-stressed half-slumber. Reality sets in. You realize you've done it again—blown it with your friends . . . again. You swore you wouldn't forget the dinner plans tonight, and you didn't really. . . . You just had no idea it had gotten to be so late so soon. You apologize profusely and begin gathering your belongings even before you hang up. One final "save" command on the screen, and you rush off into the night, bawling tires out of the parking lot like a sixteen-year-old kid.

After dinner later that night, you lie in bed thinking of all the work you still have to do and feeling guilty for letting your friends down. If only there were some way to get it all done and still be the fun-loving person you used to be. If only the stress would level off just a little bit. If only . . .

Scenes like this one play out in the lives of countless twentys all over the country who are 100 percent dedicated to their work but still want to have a life aside from it. They try to balance the demands of an emerging career with their desire to have a fun social life. The stakes are high because they feel like only half a person if either of these two warring forces is ignored.

It doesn't have to be this way! Make up your mind to change things. Here are some tips:

KNOW YOUR LIMITS
And don't just *know* them, but make the commitment not to exceed them. Nearly everyone can overextend for a while, but working beyond your margin on a continual basis will leave you feeling out of control and overwhelmed. When that happens, even the work you do manage to complete will not be your best.

COMMUNICATE YOUR LIMITS
This will be especially hard for you overachievers out there. No one likes to admit failure or weakness. But realizing your true limits and committing yourself to respecting them is not failure or weakness at all. In fact, it's a sign of great strength! Be assertive, confident, and courageous enough to express the limitations of your time, resources, and energy both in and out of the office.

GUARD SOME TIME AS OFF-LIMITS
Everyone needs some R & R now and then. If you find yourself working all weekend *every* weekend or late into the night *every* night, you need to set aside some time for rejuvenation. Do things you just *like* to do instead of only what you *need* to do. Hey, even God rested!

NETWORK
WITH PEOPLE WHO
ARE SMARTER THAN YOU

ARE YOU SICK OF PEOPLE HARPING on you about networking? You can roll your eyes if you want to, but it's a proven fact that most people get places in life by building relationships with influential people. This isn't nuclear physics, you guys. Throughout your life—whether you're twenty-two or seventy-two—the relationships you build might very well better your career and ultimately your life.

You can certainly choose not to network if you want to, but realistically if you want to be more successful, more knowledgeable, and more competitive in today's fast-paced work environment, you've gotta learn how to meet the right people. Heck, if you want a job, you have to get out there and make yourself known. But don't fret—networking is not as hard as some make it out to be. You simply need a little gumption and a desire to learn. Follow these seven networking principles, and you'll be climbing the career ladder in no time:

❶ KNOW WHO'S IN THE ROOM.
As the old saying goes, "Knowledge is power." It doesn't matter if you're at a friend's party, at a work get-together, on vacation, or in church—don't be afraid to introduce yourself to someone you don't know. Don't be obnoxious about it, but remember that it never hurts to just put your hand out and say hello.

❷ BEGIN WITH THOSE YOU KNOW BEST.
Your family and friends may have many contacts you can network with. If your father knows a man who knows the cousin of the CEO of Apple, you might have an in.

❸ LET THE OTHER PERSON DO MOST OF THE TALKING.
Play it cool. Most influencers have no trouble talking about themselves and what they've accomplished. Now is not the time to bore them with too much of your story. Find out as much as you can about them.

❹ THINK OF YOUR JOB SEARCH AS A PERSONAL RESEARCH PROJECT ON A COMPELLING SUBJECT—YOUR OWN FUTURE.
With that attitude, you'll find it easier to collect critical information and ideas.

❺ GET THE DIGITS.
When you meet people you'd like to add to your contact list, make sure you ask for their card or contact information. Ask them if they'd mind if you called or e-mailed them sometime. And follow up by getting in touch within two or three days.

❻ TAKE THEM OUT FOR A CUP OF COFFEE.
Nine times out of ten, people of influence are willing to lend their time to help others be successful. So if you've made a connection you think can help you go further, invite that person out for a cup of coffee or lunch. And be sure to pick up the bill!

❼ BE PREPARED.
Wherever you go, take business cards with you. You never know whom you might meet. Remember, the one who is prepared stands out in a crowd!

1 BE AWARE OF YOUR ENVIRONMENT! Don't be naïve enough to think that you can trust everyone. Of course, be involved—just be smart about it.

2 DON'T GOSSIP. Boy, is gossip a fun way to pass the time—but it can be deadly to your career. Before you even step foot into the office, make a point not to participate in office slander, no matter how innocent it seems. Remember: The person who gossips *to* you will also gossip *about* you.

3 RESIST THE TEMPTATION TO BE JEALOUS. You're going to meet people at the office who will quickly move up the ladder or receive preferential treatment for seemingly no reason at all. A surefire way to lose at office politics is to reveal your jealous spirit. Even if you are jealous, *never* let it show. At the very first sign, take jealous thoughts captive and replace them with happy ones!

4 GIVE CREDIT WHERE CREDIT IS DUE. Never take credit for someone else's work. If you're the supervisor, let your employees have some credit. If you're the low man in the office, make your supervisor look like the best boss in the world. Either way, you'll be seen as an honest, humble individual. And honesty and humility are always good things.

5 TAKE THE HIGH ROAD. So your boss has just taken all the credit for your hard work. It stinks, doesn't it? But don't gripe and complain about it. A good attitude always wins in the end.

6 PERIODICALLY ASK YOUR BOSS FOR ADVICE. Your boss will more than likely see you as a protégé or ally. And if situations arise, she's more apt to have your back down the road.

7 LOOK FOR WAYS TO BE ENCOURAGING AND HELPFUL. Stay late and help your colleague finish her project. Send a handwritten thank-you note to those who stayed late to help you. Or bring homemade cookies to the office. In other words, give your colleagues reason to love you.

8 BE VISIBLE. It's one thing to be humble; it's another to be invisible. Don't be afraid to volunteer to lead the important task. You may have to put in extra hours to get the work done, but your employer will take notice of you and your hard work. You can't beat that kind of politicking.

9 PRAY. Do not underestimate the power of prayer in the workplace. God desires for his children to be good representations of him, so ask him for wisdom and guidance.

PLAY OFFICE POLITICS AND *WIN!*

No matter where you work, office politics exist. Sadly, some offices are almost as bad as the reality TV show *Survivor* in that you have to choose who you'll trust, who you'll dismiss, who you'll form alliances with, and who you'll stay far away from. Who has time for that? Here's an office-politics game plan for you to follow. When you're positive, you always win!

GIFT-GIVING @ WORK

LIFE EVENTS ADD UP when coworkers experience birthdays, weddings, babies, promotions, and retirements. These should be times of joy and celebration, but oh the pain and embarrassment of a gift-giving snafu! How could you have known your neighbor in the next cubicle was giving you a Rolex when you bought him a shiny new Bic pen? Here's some advice to save you from utter humiliation the next time a gift-giving opportunity rolls around:

WHO IS APPROPRIATE?

Holidays are the most popular occasions for gift giving. You can give just about anybody a small gift without much ado during the Christmas season. Other times during the year are a bit trickier. Generally, subordinates do not give gifts to their superiors and superiors do not give personal gifts to subordinates. Close work friends are obviously acceptable recipients. A good rule of thumb is not to give a gift to someone if you wouldn't want anyone else in the office to know about it.

WHAT OCCASIONS ARE APPROPRIATE?

Christmas is always nice and safe, but your gift may have a better chance of getting noticed if you send it as a birthday, congratulations, or thank-you gift. Personal milestones such as weddings, births, and retirements are other suitable occasions. Be sure to be consistent, though. If you give several co-workers a birthday gift, try to do something equally nice for everyone else's big day too.

WHAT GIFTS ARE APPROPRIATE?

Office gifts and accessories are the most conventional options for business situations. Pens, portfolios, and calendars are nice standbys. Anything baked or homemade will always be appreciated and meaningful. More personal items are nice too, but proceed with much caution and common sense. And remember to wrap carefully—presentation is as important as content!

CAN YOU SAY "OUCH!"?

According to a study by the Commonwealth Fund, forty percent of recent graduates lived without health insurance for several months after graduation. Bad idea when a battle with pneumonia can cost about $16,000 and a one-day stay in the hospital costs more than $3,000.

WORK-A-HOLIC

A recent study found that men who work sixty hours a week are twice as likely to have a heart attack as those who work only forty hours each week.

DID YOU KNOW?

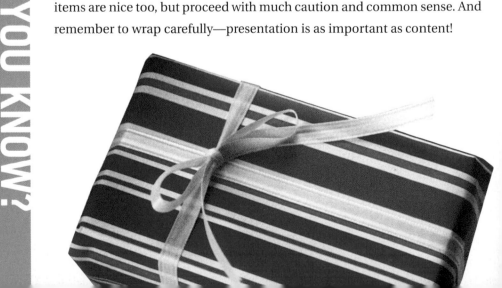

WORK QUOTES "

Maurice: "Oh yeah, I started out mopping the floor just like you guys. Then I moved up to washing lettuces. Now I'm working the fat fryer. Pretty soon I'll make assistant manager, and that's when the big bucks start rolling in."

—*Coming to America* (1988)

"When your work speaks for itself, don't interrupt."

—*Henry L. Kaiser*

BORING MEETINGS BE GONE!

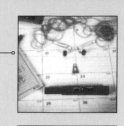

Employees today spend hours upon hours in meetings. Sometimes the meetings are so frequent that you can't even get your work done in between meeting times. You have to schedule meetings just to sit down and schedule meetings!

Next time you're in charge, bring along these proven meeting enhancers for improved energy, creativity, and attitude:

REFRESHMENTS AND DRINK—HAPPY STOMACHS MEAN HAPPY BRAINS!

HARD CANDY—BUSY MOUTHS DON'T TALK AS MUCH!

CREATIVE TOYS LIKE A SLINKY, HACKY SACK, PLAY-DOH, OR SILLY PUTTY—SURE-FIRE BOREDOM BUSTERS!

COLORED STICKY NOTES—WRITE DOWN EACH GREAT IDEA AND PLACE IT IN FRONT OF THE BIG THINKER.

AN ALARM CLOCK—EVERYONE'S HAPPY WHEN MEETINGS END ON TIME!

If you want to quit your job but still keep your current employer as a future reference, you're going to need to extend a little grace. Here are a couple things to remember:

AVOID BURNING ANY BRIDGES
You never know when you might need your old job (*gasp*) back, so make sure you put in plenty of notice and maintain a positive attitude until the last day and beyond.

AVOID BADMOUTHING YOUR WORKPLACE
Fellow employees talk, so if you're a bit disgruntled, it's best not to let on. Instead, focus on the things and people you've appreciated in your workplace.

QUITTING WITH GRACE

INSPIRING WORDS FROM BENJAMIN FRANKLIN

(He was the smart dude who discovered electricity in the eighteenth century.)

" A GOOD CONSCIENCE IS A CONTINUAL CHRISTMAS. // HONESTY IS THE BEST POLICY. // IT IS THE WORKING MAN WHO IS THE HAPPY MAN. IT IS THE IDLE MAN WHO IS THE MISERABLE MAN. // IF PASSION DRIVES YOU, LET REASON HOLD THE REINS. // TO BE HUMBLE TO SUPERIORS IS DUTY, TO EQUALS COURTESY, TO INFERIORS NOBLENESS. // THE USE OF MONEY IS ALL THE ADVANTAGE THERE IS IN HAVING IT. // EITHER WRITE SOMETHING WORTH READING OR DO SOMETHING WORTH WRITING. // HIDE NOT YOUR TALENTS, THEY FOR USE WERE MADE. WHAT'S A SUNDIAL IN THE SHADE? // IF YOU WOULD BE LOVED, LOVE AND BE LOVABLE. "

FAITH—AN INTRODUCTION

ON HIS WAY TO HIS FIFTH SPEAKING ENGAGEMENT OF THE DAY, ANTHONY HAD STOPPED AT A CONVENIENCE STORE AND POURED HIMSELF AN XXL CUP OF CARBONATION. SLURPING THE LAST BIT THROUGH THE STRAW, HE PARKED THE CAR IN THE HIGH SCHOOL PARKING LOT. HE MOUNTED THE PLATFORM AND WAS HALFWAY THROUGH HIS SECOND POINT WHEN HE REALIZED THE XXL SODA MIGHT NOT HAVE BEEN THE BEST IDEA. CUTTING HIS TALK SHORT, HE RAN DOWN THE AISLE, OUT THE BACK DOOR, AND INTO THE NEAREST RESTROOM. THE STALL DOOR HAD JUST SLAMMED SHUT WHEN HE HEARD FEMALE VOICES NEARBY. THE SOUNDS OF HAIR SPRAY AND RANDOM COMMENTS ABOUT JUDE LAW CONFIRMED HIS SUSPICIONS EVEN BEFORE HE STOOD ON THE PORCELAIN STEP STOOL TO PEER OVER THE STALL. HE CHECKED THE LATCH ON HIS STALL, BUT IT WAS BROKEN. IF ONE OF THE GIRLS OPENED THE DOOR, HE WOULD SUDDENLY BE STARRING IN HIS OWN MOTION PICTURE: *CROUCHING SPEAKER, HIDDEN PERVERT.* ANTHONY CROUCHED ON THE STOOL UNTIL THE GIRLS LEFT. THINKING HE HAD GOTTEN AWAY UNNOTICED, HE STEPPED INTO THE HALL . . . WHERE A GROUP OF GIRLS IMMEDIATELY OFFERED UP AN EMBARRASSING ROUND OF APPLAUSE. DESPITE THE UNFORTUNATE BATHROOM EPISODE CUTTING HIS TALK SHORT, SEVERAL PEOPLE TOLD HIM LATER HOW GOD HAD USED HIS TALK THAT EVENING IN THEIR LIVES. GO FIGURE. THE POINT IS THAT DURING OUR DUMB TIMES, AND ESPECIALLY DURING AWKWARD AND EMBARRASSING TIMES, WHETHER WE KNOW IT OR NOT, GOD IS AT WORK. HE'S ALWAYS AT WORK IN US, REGARDLESS OF THE CIRCUMSTANCES OF LIFE WE FACE, EVEN AFTER DRINKING AN EIGHTY-SIX-OUNCE MEGA GULP. WHEN WE WERE KIDS, OUR RESPONSIBILITIES WERE LIMITED TO HOME, SCHOOL, CHURCH, AND PERHAPS A JOB. LIKE NO OTHER TIME, OUR TWENTYS HOLD THE PROMISE OF SOME OF LIFE'S BEST POSSIBILITIES. NOT ONLY DO WE GET OUR FIRST "SERIOUS MONEY" JOB (HOPEFULLY), BUT WE ALSO SPEND THESE YEARS LEARNING HOW TO DEAL WITH THE HARSH REALITIES OF LIFE. SURE, WE'RE GOING TO MAKE MISTAKES AND DO DUMB THINGS. WHAT WE BELIEVE ABOUT GOD, THE BIBLE, JESUS, THE CHURCH, AND OTHER PEOPLE PLAYS A HUGE PART IN OUR DECISIONS AND EXPERIENCES, AS WELL AS THE WAY WE REACT AND REGROUP AFTER GOOFING UP. MANY TWENTYS ASK SUCH QUESTIONS AS, WHY AM I HERE AND HOW CAN I MAKE THE MOST OUT OF MY LIFE?; HOW DO I DISCOVER WHAT REALLY MATTERS?; WHAT AND WHO CAN I DEPEND ON?; AND, WHAT IS THE RIGHT WAY OF LIVING AND WHO MAKES IT SO? WE WON'T FINISH OUR FAITH JOURNEY OVERNIGHT. WE NEED TO BE OPEN TO NEW THOUGHTS AND FRESH CHALLENGES THAT WILL TAKE US TO PLACES WE NEVER DREAMED POSSIBLE. THE JOURNEY IS NOT THE EASIEST, BUT GOD MEETS US WITH WISDOM AND STRENGTH AT EVERY DECISION POINT ALONG THE WAY. HE WANTS US TO TURN TO HIM SO THAT TOGETHER WE CAN IMPACT OUR WORLD FOR CHRIST. OUR FAITH IMPACTS THE WAY WE WORSHIP, THE WAY WE PRAY, THE WAY WE PERCEIVE OTHERS, AND THE WAY WE MAKE CHOICES. FAITH HELPS US DISCOVER THE POWER THAT GOD'S WORD BRINGS INTO OUR LIVES. FAITH BRINGS CHANGE IN THE WORLD AROUND US THROUGH THE CHOICES WE MAKE. THE TWENTYS DECADE IS FILLED WITH AMAZING OPPORTUNITIES AND CHALLENGES. OUR DREAMS SHARPEN, OUR INTENSITY BUILDS, OUR POTENTIAL IS DISCOVERED, AND OUR FAITH TAKES SHAPE. THESE ARE THE YEARS THAT WILL DETERMINE THE DIRECTION OF OUR LIVES.

FAITH

BELIEF IN CHRIST BRINGS BENEFITS

Have you heard the story about the guy who was dressed in a banana suit when he found Christ? No joke. While in college, he landed a job dressing up like a seven-foot banana and handing out fruit samples in a grocery store. "One day after my shift," he says, "I put a couple candy bars in my banana suit. I didn't have anything to eat at home. They must have been watching on the in-store security camera because when I stepped outside, the store manager busted me and called the police." Picture the scene: a seven-foot banana handcuffed and stuffed in the backseat of a police cruiser! As the banana tells it, "They took me to the police station, fingerprinted me, and stood me in a lineup." (*Criminal, criminal, criminal, banana, criminal. . . .*) "It was at that moment, standing there in the lineup, that I realized I needed Jesus to be my Savior."

Every follower of Christ has a unique story of the day they connected with Jesus. But did you know that the Bible boldly declares that four things happen to all of us when we connect with the life of Christ? Consider the following four points all cleverly beginning with the letter *f*. Then go eat a banana. You look like you could use the potassium.

FOREVER When we connect with Christ, our eternity is forever settled. The connection Christ forges with each of us is never ending, unbreakable, and forever. Everyone he connects with will always and forever be with him. "God has said, 'I will never fail you. I will never abandon you'" (Hebrews 13:5).

FAMILY When we connect with Christ, we are instantly transformed into full and complete sons and daughters of God. We receive a new position. Forever and always we are a part of God's eternal family.

FORGIVENESS In Christ, every mistake, failure, and sin has been removed so we are free to lift our heads in confidence. God's Word says, "As far as the east is from the west, so far has He removed our transgressions from us" (Psalm 103:12, NASB).

FREEDOM Once we connect to the life of Christ, we are free to be everything God created us to be. The best life has to offer now spreads out in front of us. Jesus said, "If the Son sets you free, you are truly free" (John 8:36).

Regardless of the way we discover our need for Christ, these four results are the common experiences of every believer. If you have already linked your life to Christ, let the benefits of this life become real to you. If you're not yet connected with Christ, now is the best time to stop living your way and start life anew.

"The outcome of your faith [is] the salvation of your souls" (1 Peter 1:9, NASB).

Have you heard the story about the guy who was dressed in a banana suit when he found Christ?

FAITH QUOTES
"You can give without loving, but you cannot love without giving."
—*Robert Louis Stevenson*

Dealing with DOUBT

Imagine the following scenarios. . . .

You prayed earnestly about whether to take the job. All the doors opened and you sensed God's peace, so you accepted the position and went to work. But lately you can't help wondering if this is really where you're supposed to be. You hope you aren't out of God's will, but how can you be sure?

You've always been careful to seek God in every area of your dating life. You were certain he was giving you the green light with this one. But lately you've been wondering if you're making a mistake. What if you didn't hear him correctly?

You know you have a real, personal, intimate relationship with Christ. You don't doubt for one second that he is who he says he is. But you begged him not to let your grandmother die, and he did anyway. You question his goodness . . . and immediately feel guilty for doing so.

Doubts creep in. You try to ignore them, but they keep nagging. You're a Christian. You aren't supposed to have doubts! You're supposed to be the one who has it all together. What's wrong with you? How dare you doubt God!

Relax. Everyone has doubts at some point . . . at many points, actually. It doesn't mean you aren't a real believer. The opposite of belief is *unbelief*, not doubt. And you're a hypocrite only if you try to deny that you ever have doubts like the rest of us.

WHEN YOU FIND YOURSELF STRUGGLING WITH DOUBTS, CONSIDER DOING THE FOLLOWING:

ACKNOWLEDGE THE DOUBT. Pretending it's not there will not help. And this is *so* much worse than trying to pretend you don't have a unibrow. Allow yourself the freedom to think through your questions. And if you have a unibrow, wax it, baby!

BE HONEST WITH GOD. Tell him what you feel. He knows every little thing you're thinking anyway, so you might as well 'fess up and ask him to walk through the valley of the shadow of doubt with you.

SEEK COUNSEL. Spend extra time in God's Word. Use a concordance to find passages that deal with your particular situation. Enlist the advice and prayers of wise, trusted friends. Just don't ask the friend who keeps telling you that a unibrow is completely okay. That person is not your friend.

STICK WITH WHAT YOU KNOW. You do not know everything there is to know about God and life. You may not ever know the answers to your questions. But that's what faith is for. Authentic faith chooses to trust, with or without understanding. Run back to the things you do know about God. Make a list of truths you absolutely believe without any doubt, and then revisit your question in light of that list. And please, please, please include an anti-unibrow truth in there somewhere.

Hold on to what you know with all you've got, and before long the doubts will subside. (And then new ones will come. It's a vicious cycle!) The key is to just work through the doubts as they come. Don't ignore them. Don't beat yourself up about them. Give them attention and thought, but don't constantly dwell on them. Dwell on him.

God is not going to lose control of the cosmos or suddenly become unable to work in or through you just because you misinterpret his will for your life. "The Lord's plans stand firm forever; his intentions can never be shaken" (Psalm 33:11). And he is not afraid of your questions. His Word is truth and he is perfect, so ask away! Working through the doubt cycle will make you stronger in your faith when all is said and done.

PRAY LIKE JESUS PRAYED

MANY PEOPLE DON'T PRAY. Maybe you're one of those people—you don't understand prayer, you don't know how to pray, and you don't know what to expect when you do pray. You're *really* high maintenance, aren't you? *Just kidding.* But here's the deal: If you're praying for God to help you humbly serve him *and* to make you famous, you're praying the wrong way. If you're praying for your favorite soap stars, really—what's the point? If you're praying for God to give you a limber neck because you didn't study for the test, you might as well pray, too, that he doesn't seat you next to someone dumb.

Jesus told us to pray the way he prayed: "Our Father who is in heaven . . . Your kingdom come. Your will be done, on earth as it is in heaven" (Matthew 6:9-10, NASB). That kind of prayer is powerful and productive.

HERE ARE FOUR WAYS TO MAKE SURE YOUR PRAYERS GET RESULTS:

PRAY WITH CONVICTION.
Pray with the personal conviction that God is actually capable of doing what you ask him to do. *Hello?* He's God. We must believe that he is not only capable but also *willing* to respond to our requests. Prayer is not a superstition; it is certain confidence that our words carry weight with God. Dare to believe that what Jesus told us to do really will bring about change in our world.

PRAY WITH THE BIBLE IN MIND.
God's answers to prayer are always in harmony with the Bible. The more familiar we are with God's Word, the more effective our prayers will be. Read Jesus' prayers in the New Testament or David's prayers in the Psalms and try using their words in your own conversations with God. You'll be surprised at how powerful it can be to pray God's Word.

BE SPECIFIC.
Don't just pray for God to "bless your family"—ask him to curb your dad's road rage or heal your grandma's bunion. *(Yuck, bunions are so gross.)* But the point is this: Be specific! How will you know whether God has answered your prayer if you don't even truly know what you've been praying for? Trust God enough to stop generalizing and tell him what's *really* on your mind. Specific prayers get specific answers.

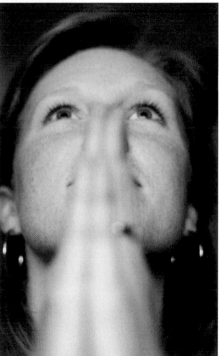

EXPECT AN ANSWER.
When you pray, anticipate the answer. Jesus said, "Keep on asking, and you will receive what you ask for" (Matthew 7:7). You're not just shooting up a prayer flare hoping that God sees it. You're talking to God about what's on your heart. He cares, and he will answer. Our world can only be saved by the free expression and exercise of God's will. When you pray, pray as Jesus said—that God's will would come and be experienced in our lives as it is in heaven.

WORLDVIEW COMPARISON CHART

		REALITY	MAN	TRUTH	VALUES
NATURALISM	ATHEISM AGNOSTICISM EXISTENTIALISM	The material universe is all that exists. Reality is "one-dimensional." There is no such thing as a soul or a spirit. Everything can be explained on the basis of natural law.	Man is the chance product of a biological process of evolution. Man is entirely material. The human species will one day pass out of existence.	Truth is usually understood as scientific proof. Only that which can be observed with the five senses is accepted as real or true.	No objective values or morals exist. Morals are individual preferences or socially useful behaviors. Even social morals are subject to evolution and change.
PANTHEISM	HINDUISM TAOISM BUDDHISM NEW AGE CONSCIOUSNESS	Only the spiritual dimension exists. All else is illusion, maya. Spiritual reality, Brahman, is eternal, impersonal, and unknowable. It is possible to say that everything is a part of God, or that God is in everything and everyone.	Man is one with ultimate reality. Thus man is spiritual, eternal, and impersonal. Man's belief that he is an individual is illusion.	Truth is an experience of unity with "the one-ness" of the universe. Truth is beyond all rational description. Rational thought as it is understood in the West cannot show us reality.	Because ultimate reality is impersonal, many pantheistic thinkers believe that there is no real distinction between good and evil. Instead, "unenlightened" behavior is that which fails to understand essential unity.
THEISM	CHRISTIANITY ISLAM JUDAISM	An infinite, personal God exists. He created a finite, material world. Reality is both material and spiritual. The universe as we know it had a beginning and will have an end.	Humankind is the unique creation of God. People were created "in the image of God," which means that we are personal, eternal, spiritual, and biological.	Truth about God is known through revelation. Truth about the material world is gained via revelation and the five senses in conjunction with rational thought.	Moral values are the objective expression of an absolute moral being.
POLYTHEISM	THOUSANDS OF RELIGIONS	The world is populated by spirit beings who govern what goes on. Gods and demons are the real reason behind "natural" events. Material things are real, but they have spirits associated with them.	Man is a creation of the gods like the rest of the creatures on earth. Often, tribes or races have a special relationship with some gods who protect them and can punish them.	Truth about the natural world is discovered through the shaman figure who has visions telling him what the gods and demons are doing and how they feel.	Moral values take the form of taboos, which are things that irritate or anger various spirits. These taboos are different from the idea of "good and evil" because it is just as important to avoid irritating evil spirits as it is good ones.
POSTMODERNISM		Reality must be interpreted through our language and cultural "paradigm." Therefore, reality is "socially constructed."	Humans are nodes in a cultural reality – they are a product of their social setting. The idea that people are autonomous and free is a myth.	Truths are mental constructs meaningful to individuals within a particular cultural paradigm. They do not apply to other paradigms. Truth is relative to one's culture.	Values are part of our social paradigms as well. Tolerance, freedom of expression, inclusion, and refusal to claim to have the answers are the only universal values.

This chart is adapted from *Christianity: The Faith That Makes Sense* by Dennis McCallum (Tyndale House Publishers, 1992).

> "A brick wants to belong to something greater than itself."

DUMB EXCUSES FOR NOT SERVING

It was the beginning of the fall semester, and Architecture 101 had filled room 307A to capacity. In walked a man with silver-grey hair, wearing a weathered blue work shirt, British-made khakis, and brown Chukka boots. When he threw his well worn leather satchel on the desk, it landed with a heavy thud, but not the thud of books. All the students turned to look as the teacher unsnapped the flap of the satchel. He removed an ancient brick and held it high over his head with one hand.

"This is a brick," he said. Then with his other hand, he pointed to a series of lithographs capturing the majesty of cathedrals and mansions that hung just behind him. "These are constructed of bricks. A brick wants to belong to something greater than itself. The job of the architect is to figure out where the bricks belong. Let's get started."

Like bricks, believers belong to something greater than ourselves. We belong to the Kingdom of God, and we have a purpose to fulfill: that of service. We discover our true sense of value and belonging when we serve. But so many believers don't serve. They have excuses, but God has answers.

"WHATEVER I MIGHT DO WON'T BE ENOUGH—IT WON'T MAKE A DIFFERENCE."

Gosh, don't be such a whiner. This is simply *fear* trying to convince us that with so many things wrong in the world our small efforts will have little to no impact. "For God has not given us a spirit of timidity, but of power and love and discipline" (2 Timothy 1:7, NASB). Don't let fear dominate you. Expect everything you do for God to make a difference.

"I DON'T KNOW IF I CAN DO IT."

This is the *worst* excuse, but all of us have said it at one time or another. This is *risk* trying to convince us to choose the security of our plans over God's plans. But we're at the greatest risk when we choose to be separated from God's plans. Someday Jesus is going to judge the world, and we'll have to give an account for what we did and didn't do (Matthew 25:14-30). Be bold with the abilities God has given you. You will give an account for them. Be bold, quit waiting, jump out, and serve.

"THERE ARE OTHERS WHO CAN DO IT BETTER."

This is *comparison* telling us that we are somehow substandard Christians. The Bible says: "There are different kinds of spiritual gifts, but the same Spirit is the source of them all. There are different kinds of service, but we serve the same Lord. God works in different ways, but it is the same God who does the work in all of us" (1 Corinthians 12:4-6). God wants you to use what he's given you—don't worry about how you might compare to other people. He has different plans for them.

"I KNOW IT'S IMPORTANT, BUT IT'S NOT *MY* PROBLEM."

Okay, if you're saying this one you're just plain selfish. No, really, admit it—you're selfish. Come on, people. The heart of God has been placed within us, and his heart is all over service. "Work hard so you can present yourself to God and receive his approval. Be a good worker, one who does not need to be ashamed and who correctly explains the word of truth" (2 Timothy 2:15). The call to serve is not self-made—it is born in the heart and mind of God. He has called every believer to be an active part of building his Kingdom.

Service is as much a part of who we are in Christ as bricks are part of quality construction. We are Christ's living stones vitally connected to the construction of his Kingdom. We have both position and power in the service we are called to do. Let's get started. • • • • • • • • • • • • • • • •

EVERY CHRISTIAN NEEDS A LOCAL CHURCH

You've probably heard a lot of people say that church membership is optional. But regardless of how popular this opinion is, it simply isn't taught in Scripture.

There are a number of passages that instruct all believers to be dynamically connected to a local faith community. The Bible calls this group the body of Christ, which reinforces how important it is to belong to a church. A body must have all its parts in order to be whole—the same is true of the body of Christ. Every local community of faith needs the completeness believers bring to it.

First Corinthians 12:14-26 is perhaps the most powerful passage of Scripture explaining why every Christian should belong to a church.

The church is an important part of God's plan for all believers because in the church we discover the fullness of who Christ made us to be. We truly find ourselves when we look for our identity in Christ in the context of the local church.

In 1 Corinthians, Paul describes every church member as a different part of the body. Hands, eyes, feet, and ears all work together to accomplish God's purposes on earth. Each member holds a significant position in the body. At the same time, no member is more important than another. Each of us is a vital part of the body, and we must all work together to show God to the world.

As members of the body of Christ, our choices and actions impact the other members. The Scripture teaches us that when one member of the body is hurt, the other members are hurt too. This doesn't necessarily mean that we feel the same pain. It does mean that when one member falls short in fulfilling its role, the rest of the body doesn't function as well as it should.

If the whole body suffers when one part comes up short, how does it affect the body when countless members are completely absent from the ranks of membership? We need to be connected to the community of faith. We need the church. According to Scripture, it's not optional; it's necessary to our fulfilling God's plans and purposes in the world.

"Let us consider how to stimulate one another to love and good deeds, not forsaking our own assembling together, as is the habit of some, but encouraging one another" (Hebrews 10:24-25, NASB).

KEY WORD: *Worship*

Should worship music be upbeat or slow? Can we raise our hands and dance in the aisles, or should we be more reserved? Is genuine worship supposed to feel a certain way? How will we know when we have truly worshipped?

SPIRIT

Worship is so often misunderstood. There's way too much mystery surrounding something that is completely central to our Christian experience. Scripture teaches us that genuine worship is balanced by two things: spirit and truth. John 4:1-26 gives an account of Jesus talking with a woman beside a well. While visiting with this woman, Jesus reveals the two things that balance worship: "True worshipers will worship the Father in spirit and truth; for such people the Father seeks to be His worshipers" (John 4:23, NASB).

We worship in spirit. Worship is not an intense set of mental gymnastics. It's an authentic experience with God. It's as real as two people sitting down over a cup of coffee and sharing the deepest parts of their hearts with each other. They each give part of themselves away and they each take something of the other away when they leave.

Not only do we walk away from worship with deep personal benefits, but we also experience corporate benefits from worship. Worshipping with others gives us a unique connection with our brothers and sisters in Christ. And it keeps the church focused on God's love and purposes.

TRUTH

Jesus said that we will worship God in truth. We focus our worship on the things the Bible tells us that Jesus did while he was on earth—his birth, life, death and burial, resurrection, and return to heaven. Jesus is always the subject and the object of our worship.

Worship exposes who we really are to the purity and perfection of God. It makes us vulnerable. In this exposed position, God gently and lovingly shapes our character. He changes us on the inside so our behavior can also change.

Worship connects us to the person of God. It intensifies our intimacy with him. It places us in direct contact with the Creator and giver of life. In our worship connection, we will experience firsthand the presence of God.

SMALL: ME, MINE, YOU, YOURS, US, OURS, THEM, AND THEIRS. FINITE, TEMPORARY, LIMITED, PASSING, BRIEF, FIXED, NARROW, AND RESTRICTED. PICTURE, PORTRAIT, IMAGE, COPY, PHOTO, IMITATION, REPRODUCTION, AND REPRESENTATIVE. EMPTY, UNFILLED, BARE, BLANK, VACANT, PLAIN, UNOCCUPIED, AND NAKED.

SEE THE BIGGER PICTURE
CRAVE THE BIGGER PICTURE

BIG: MEANING, SIGNIFICANCE, IMPORTANCE, PURPOSE, VALUE, WORTH, INTENTION, AND SENSE. INFINITE, BOUNDLESS, VAST, COSMIC, CEASELESS, PERPETUAL, UNENDING, AND PERMANENT. NEED, REQUIRE, NECESSITATE, DEMAND, INSIST, CRAVE, DESIRE, AND YEARN. FULFILLED, SATISFIED, CONTENTED, RELAXED, PEACEFUL, UNDISTURBED, QUIET, AND CONFIDENT.

LIFE FOUND IN OURSELVES IS SMALL.

LIFE FOUND IN GOD IS BIGGER THAN WE EVER COULD IMAGINE.

YOUR
WORSHIP GUIDE

// WHAT YOUR POSTURE SAYS ABOUT YOUR WORSHIP

1 You're most likely shy. You like keeping to yourself. Praise and worship time at church is a bit awkward for you.

4 You're open, teachable, and at ease. You're probably quite comfortable with what you know about God. This is also a good position for anyone who is on the worship dance team.

2 You're noncommittal, tentative, and cautious—not very much fun to hang around, really. And you need to stop being so concerned about what someone else might think about you. God already knows your heart, bro.

5 Oh, we've got you pegged, bro. You're uninhibited, celebratory— perhaps even an exhibitionist. You are quick to declare for all to see that God rules... and it's good to know that you wear deodorant to church.

3 You *hate* extremes. You're just comfortable being in the "good hands" of God.

6 You're right where we all need to be. You're reverent and humble. You recognize the authority, power, and presence of God.

CHOICE Is the Most Important Word

Our entire life is built around one word: *choice*. We've all been given the power to choose. That's what separates us from the animal kingdom—that and the fact that we're not afraid of vacuum cleaners and most of us don't run around on all fours.

Everything in life comes down to choice. When someone cuts us off in traffic, some of us choose to develop a spontaneous case of Tourette's syndrome—calling out whatever foul words come to our lips. Some of us choose to smoke. If you say you didn't know it was bad for you, you're lying through your trachea. Who would run into a burning building, take a few deep breaths, and then choke, "I couldn't help myself"? And then there are the choices we make about sex and dating. Some twentys say, "I don't know how we ended up having sex—it just happened." Did they really just watch as their clothes unbuckled, unsnapped, unbuttoned, and unzipped themselves? Yeah, right. Or maybe you've heard people say, "You can't help who you fall in love with." You may have feelings that surprise you, but don't you get to choose what to do with those feelings and whether or not to let them grow?

The life we live is the sum total of the choices we make. God created life and knows better than anyone how to make it work. It's a mystery that he's all too willing to share . . . if we make the choice to ask.

TIPS FOR MAKING GOOD CHOICES:

GET TO KNOW THE WISDOM OF SCRIPTURE. Start reading the Proverbs. There is more practical truth in those thirty-one chapters than you could use in a lifetime.

GET CLOSE TO ONE OR TWO GODLY PEOPLE. Before making a critical decision, talk it over with these people . . . and then listen to what they have to say. Consider their advice before making your final decision.

GET REAL WITH YOURSELF. Sometimes it's easier to fool yourself into doing something stupid than it is to fool anyone else. One of the key indicators that you're growing up is that you stop lying to yourself. Look in the mirror and ask yourself if the choice you're making is the best one.

GET REAL WITH GOD. Pray about your choices . . . over a period of days or even weeks. Few choices in life have to be made immediately. Pray about them and listen for what God has to say. The reason you don't hear from God is because you're not listening all that well.

FAITH QUOTES

"Christ has no body now but yours, no hands, no feet, on earth but yours. You are the eyes through which He looks compassion on this world. Yours are the feet with which He walks to do good. You are the hands with which He blesses all the world."
—*Saint Teresa of Avila*

AUTHORITY MATTERS

"I'M AN ADULT NOW. I DON'T NEED YOU TELLING ME WHEN TO BE HOME AND WHEN TO GO TO BED."

"MY TEACHER IS A COMPLETE GOOF. IF HE KNEW HOW TO TEACH I WOULDN'T BE MAKING A D IN HIS CLASS."

"I HATE MY JOB! MY BOSS HAS NO IDEA HOW THIS COMPANY NEEDS TO BE RUN."

"I'M NOT SURE I BELIEVE WHAT I WAS TAUGHT AS A CHILD ABOUT GOD. I NEED TO DISCOVER THE TRUTH ON MY OWN."

Authority is a fact of life. We may not be able to decide who has authority over us, but we *can* decide how we respond to that authority. Parents, teachers, and employers are some of the most important appointed authorities God has placed in our lives.

When we choose to respect authority, we're setting ourselves up to receive God's blessings. But when we choose to rebel against authority, well . . . let's just say things can get pretty rough when we step outside of God's will for us.

God created authority as a way to bring order into the chaos of this world. We may not always like it, but this world would be one messed-up place without it. The Bible has a lot to say about authority and how important it is for us to honor it. Jesus said, "I have been given all authority in heaven and on earth" (Matthew 28:18 NLT). He's our ultimate authority. And he'll give us the right attitude if we ask him for it.

\\\\\\\\\\\\\ **I HATE MY JOB! MY BOSS HAS NO IDEA HOW THIS COMPANY NEEDS TO BE RUN.**

WHERE THERE'S A WILL,
THERE'S A WAY ⟶

Our understanding of God's will is often fuzzy at best. We have a tendency to make discovering the will of God harder than finding a part in Donald Trump's hair. Yikes! We look for signs to validate that something we think could be God's will truly is. "I ran out of gas. What do you think God is trying to tell me?" Maybe you should have filled up with gas two exits ago. "He looked right at me. That's got to mean something." Sorry, but it means you have cilantro stuck in your teeth. "If she drives by my house, I'll know she's the one for me." Hey, man, she lives right next door to you. "It must be the will of God—we have so much in common. He lives in a house, and I live in a house. He has parents, and I have parents. . . ." We find God's will when we recognize two key principles: that the will of God is primarily about who we are, and that it addresses what we do. Throughout the Scriptures we are commanded to "love the Lord your God with all your heart" (Matthew 22:37).

Loving God draws us into greater and greater conformity with who he is. Loving him is the primary commandment in Scripture for us. Beginning with Adam and continuing to us, God has always desired intimate fellowship with mankind. He and Adam took walks together in the cool of the day. He appeared to Abraham and made promises that are still being fulfilled to this day. He declared that David was a man after his own heart. He appeared to Saul on the road to Damascus and was with John on the island of Patmos. The lives of these faithful men show us the necessity of finding our identity in continued intimacy with God. Their lives also demonstrate for us how intimacy with God helped them know how to live in agreement with God's will. The second most prominent command in Scripture is to "love your neighbor as yourself" (Matthew 22:39). The Bible is filled with instructions on the right way to live. God put them there so we'd know where to find them. As we read the Scriptures, our understanding of God's will grows. We see how those in the biblical accounts made choices both in and out of agreement with God's will. And we see both the good and the bad results of their decisions.

If we learn from these testimonies, we can avoid many of the same mistakes. We can also allow their stories to strengthen our faith. Before we know the right way to live, we must come to know who we are in Christ. This means we have to take God at his word. "You will seek me and find me when you search for me with all your heart" (Jeremiah 29:13, NASB). God waits for us to choose intimacy with him. He welcomes us with an open heart. He waits to show us who we are, and once we understand this aspect of his will, he will also reveal what we are to do.

GRAY AREAS

THERE'S ONE TWENTY-FIRST-CENTURY technology that has brought relief to egos all over the planet. It's called GPS, and it's available for any vehicle. After punching in your destination, this ingenious system not only graphically shows the correct road, but many models speak directions in a gentle, female voice. This certainly eliminates the hassle of refolding maps!

Believers are called to "walk in a manner worthy of the calling with which you have been called" (Ephesians 4:1, NASB). The believer's Genuine Positioning Strategy will guide everyone who takes advantage of it on this worthy walk. God's GPS operates according to four simple principles for every believer:

JUST BECAUSE YOU CAN DOESN'T MEAN YOU SHOULD. Sometimes no is the right answer. Just because it's there and you could do it doesn't mean you should.

JUST BECAUSE EVERYONE SAYS IT'S OKAY DOESN'T MAKE IT SO. Don't let others make your decisions for you. What does the Bible have to say about it?

JUST BECAUSE SOMEONE IN AUTHORITY DOES SOMETHING HURTFUL DOESN'T CHANGE THEIR POSITION IN YOUR LIFE. Don't put your leaders on your own private trial. Respect their authority and leave their sentencing to God.

YOU DON'T HAVE TO COMPROMISE YOUR CONVICTIONS TO GET WHAT YOU WANT. Walking worthy doesn't require personal compromise.

Apply these four principles to your decision-making, and you will find that the path ahead is one worthy of your walk. • • • • • • • • • • • •

FAITH QUOTES 66 99

"The men who followed Him were unique in their generation. They turned the world upside down because their hearts had been turned right side up. The world has never been the same."

—Billy Graham

BLAMING GOD IS NEVER THE ANSWER

Life is full of good and bad experiences. We tend to wish for more of the good and avoid as much of the bad as possible. But there are times when the negatives are completely unavoidable and we have to stand against the evil that springs up in our lives. When these times come, we must learn to cling to God's Word.

Scripture tells us to "fight the good fight" (1 Timothy 1:18, NASB), and we do that by following Christ's example in every situation we encounter. Act like Jesus would act if he were standing in our shoes. The more familiar we are with him through his Word, the better we'll know how to be Christlike in difficult situations.

When we face hard times in our own strength, we tend to react with outbursts of anger and lack of self-control. Sometimes we even resort to the silent treatment, manipulation, or unforgiveness. It takes work to respond like Christ, but his Word shows us what to do and how to do it, and his Spirit gives us the power to follow through.

And look at how Jesus responded when he was faced with the reality of his own death. He asked the Father if there was another way, but he resolved to complete his mission in life no matter how his Father answered his plea.

The apostle Paul also overflowed with the joy of Christ. It didn't matter whether Paul was in prison, hungry, shipwrecked, sleeping on the side of the road, or staying with a friend—he knew the joy of Christ. He also knew the victory the life of Christ carries with it. Because Christ lived in Paul, Paul knew that just as Jesus completed his mission so, too, could Paul.

It's important to remember that everybody's imperfect. We're all flawed and cracked. Everyone will sooner or later let us down, just as we will let others down. When that happens, turn to Christ with your questions, pain, or guilt. Don't blame him—seek him. He will give you exactly what you need.

The battle we fight is many times an unseen war. We must regularly take time to recommit ourselves to obedience to God. We must learn to ask God to help us see things through his eyes, understand the world as he does, and focus on the things that are truly important.

Good and bad times will come, and we are responsible to live the life of Christ in the midst of both. It's not only possible to do this—it's an integral part of the abundant life Jesus promised us. "We do not lose heart" (2 Corinthians 4:1, NASB).

THE CURE FOR SCREWUPS

Most of us are familiar with King David's adulterous affair with Bathsheba and the way he murdered her husband in an attempt to cover up his sin. But the Bible says that David was a man after God's own heart (1 Samuel 13:14), in spite of the terrible things he did! Most of us will never commit murder and adultery, but the lessons we learn from how David handled his situation can help us deal with our own sin:

HE ADMITTED THAT HE WAS WRONG.

When he was confronted with his sin, David confessed it to God (2 Samuel 12:13). He didn't justify the adultery or blame it on an overdose of Viagra. He didn't try to explain the murder as an adverse reaction to the codeine in his cough syrup. He admitted it and said that he was sorry . . . and he meant it.

HE UNDERSTOOD THE DIFFERENCE BETWEEN WHO HE WAS AND WHAT HE DID.

David knew that nothing he could do would ever separate him from the love of God. God's love is unconditional (Romans 8:38-39). We have a difficult time with this concept because so few of us have ever experienced love of this kind.

HE MOVED BACK TOWARD GOD.

David not only admitted that what he had done was sin but also changed the way he thought about his actions. He called what he had done *sin*, and at the same time he called himself what God called him: *loved*.

HE BELIEVED THAT GOD HAD FORGIVEN HIM.

He knew that God no longer counted his sin against him (2 Samuel 12:13). It was gone, forever forgotten. Now it was time to get on with life. There were things David and God had to do together. God was not finished with him yet.

Think of a time in your life when you blew it. Are you still dealing with it? Use David's steps back to God and put the past to rest so you and God can move forward with your future. God isn't finished with you yet.

WHY CAN'T I FEEL GOD?

If you've been in a pillow fight, you know the dull buzz that follows being pummeled by a pillowcase full of feathers. Sometimes we still get that feeling now—but without the pillows. Many of us are pummeled by the chore of daily devotions. We're so focused on reading a prescribed number of Bible verses, writing a full page in our journals, and reciting routine prayers every day that we miss out on truly interacting with God. We're treating our quiet times like homework assignments instead of seeing them as opportunities to hear from God and tell him what's truly on our hearts.

Do you feel distant from God? Like you don't really know him or are too distracted to hear his voice? We do our best to follow God, but we inevitably go through times when we can't feel God. Here are four things to consider when that happens to you:

DRYNESS Often dryness comes from unconfessed sin. We bury things we know are wrong. God calls us to transparency. Opening our souls to God detoxifies the poison of buried sin. (See 1 John 1:9.)

PRAYERLESSNESS Our lives are so busy that prayer sometimes gets as much attention as Arsenio Hall on late-night TV. Consistent prayer maintains our connectedness with God. (See 1 Thessalonians 5:17.)

TEMPTATION It's so tempting to live life our own way. We can either choose to give in to temptation, moving away from God's best for us, or we can take the escape route he always provides. (See 1 Corinthians 10:13.)

DISCOURAGEMENT While Noah was building the ark, he must have felt like he was the only person alive who was in love with God. But he persevered, and in the end he found true joy. No matter how hard things get, we always have the hope of heaven to keep us from being discouraged. (See Philippians 3:20.)

Recognize dryness, prayerlessness, temptation, and discouragement for what they are: barriers to our relationship with God. And God will remove those barriers if we ask him to. "Can anything ever separate us from Christ's love? . . . No, despite all these things, overwhelming victory is ours through Christ, who loved us" (Romans 8:35, 37).

HOW TO HEAR FROM GOD

Jesus said, "Keep on asking, and you will receive what you ask for. Keep on seeking, and you will find. Keep on knocking, and the door will be opened to you" (Matthew 7:7). Here are the top five ways we usually hear from God:

THROUGH FAMILY Parents know us best and love us most. Trust God to speak to you through your parents, even when they say things you may not want to hear.

THROUGH WISE COUNSEL You have one or two wise friends, right? Trust their proven advice after checking it against God's Word.

THROUGH THE SUPERNATURAL God sometimes speaks through dreams, desires, and visions. Exercise caution, check these against Scripture, and bounce them off your family and wise friends.

FAITH QUOTES

"To me, a faith in Jesus Christ that is not aligned with the poor, it's nothing."

—Bono, U2

"As [a man] thinketh in his heart, so is he."

—Proverbs 23:7, KJV

THROUGH CIRCUMSTANCES When God speaks, doors you couldn't open somehow seem to open all by themselves. Pay attention to where he may be leading you.

THROUGH THE BIBLE The Bible is the number one source of wisdom and good advice. Use it!

God has things to say to us, and we'll hear him if we just listen. . . . When we trust him and take action, we'll see results that are truly tremendous.

THE BIBLE IN 100 WORDS

"If only there were a simple guide that I could use, maybe then I could read the Bible and get something out of it."

GENESIS THROUGH DEUTERONOMY: LIBERATE CREATION—When you need to be set free from something.

JOSHUA THROUGH ESTHER: LOYALTY TO COMMITMENT—How to handle the tough times.

JOB THROUGH ECCLESIASTES: LONGING TO CONNECT—When you need brutal honesty with God.

THE PROPHETS: LOOKING TOWARD CHANGE—When your life needs to be transformed.

MATTHEW THROUGH JOHN: LOVE COMES—When song lyrics aren't enough.

THE EPISTLES: LIFE CONTINUES—How to do life every day.

REVELATION: LIVE COURAGEOUSLY—You're not alone or forgotten.

CHANGE THE WAY YOU THINK

The talent show was just about finished, and Chris was ready to leave. He and a few friends had plans for pizza after the show. The emcee for the night was a man who had spent countless hours helping the singles group get started. He took the stage and the microphone and announced that before they were dismissed, there was one last act. Immediately the crowd clapped and whistled out catcalls.

He reached into his jeans pocket and produced a long piece of string. The crowd quieted and the lights dimmed, leaving only the spotlight focused on the solo figure standing center stage. The music set the tone, suspenseful and mysterious. He carefully folded the string into his hand and held one end up to his nose. Inhaling sharply, he sucked the string up, swallowed twice, and then coughed three times, producing the end of string out of his mouth. The music changed into carnival music and the man began to move his hands up and down pulling the string back and forth through his head. The crowd erupted with a standing ovation. The lights came up and they were dismissed. Later at dinner Chris and his friends talked about the stunt, and Chris mentioned how it looked like the guy was flossing his mind. Chris wondered how he could take what he had just seen and apply it to his spiritual life, changing the way he thought by using "mental floss."

We all wish certain things were different in our lives—our weight, bad habits, toxic relationships. . . . We wish we spent more time in God's Word, knew more Scripture by memory, or prayed more. We've tried just about everything to change, but nothing seems to work. If we could just change the way we think, we could make some of the changes we desire. But exactly how do we change the way we think? How do we use mental floss in our own lives?

In the book of Philippians, Paul tells us how to use mental floss to change the way we think: "Finally, brethren, whatever is true, whatever is honorable, whatever is right, whatever is pure, whatever is lovely, whatever is of good repute, if there is any excellence and if anything is worthy of praise, dwell on these things" (Philippians 4:8, NASB).

It's a given in this command that we have control over our own thoughts. We can choose what we think about. Try an experiment today. Keep a mental record of how often unwholesome thoughts enter your mind and how long you allow them to remain. The key to making mental floss work is to order the impure thoughts out as soon as they enter. These types of thoughts aren't hard to recognize. As soon as you identify them, simply order them out. And then replace them with the types of good thoughts Paul describes in Philippians 4:8.

Once we understand the basics of mental floss, we can move to a more aggressive form of changing our thoughts. Use a concordance to locate verses that directly confront wrong ways of thinking. Memorizing these verses and reviewing them will intensify the effects of mental floss. Changing the way we think takes time, determination, and the right tools. Scripture is the right tool. Our continued discipline is the agent that will make changing the way we think a reality. HAPPY FLOSSING!

LIST FIVE OF THE MOST COMMON LIES YOU TELL YOURSELF. WRITE DOWN CORRESPONDING SCRIPTURES, AND WEAVE THEM IN AND OUT OF YOUR MIND ALL DAY LONG

Character is important. It's also intangible. If your dentist has week-old spinach in his teeth, keep your mouth closed. If your dietitian is five-feet-four and weighs three hundred pounds, you might want to ask a question or two. If a faith healer has a toupee . . . You get the point. That which is on the outside can make us question what's on the inside.

People with godly character display eight qualities that flow from the inside out:

❶ DO WHAT'S RIGHT.

THE GREAT

8

SPIRITUAL
QUALITIES
WE SHOULD ALL CRAVE

❷ DEAL WITH MISTAKES.

❸ DELIGHT IN HONESTY.

❹ DISCIPLINE THEIR WORDS.

❻ DELIVER THE GOODS.
(THEIR LIVES MATCH THEIR WORDS.)

❺ DEFEND THE RIGHTEOUS.

❼ DISTRIBUTE POSSESSIONS GENEROUSLY.

Keep this list handy for periodic self-inspection. Which of these eight qualities needs the most focus in your life? Do the people who know you best see these qualities as a regular part of who you are?

❽ DON'T USE OTHER PEOPLE.

THE STORY OF A CONNECTED LIFE

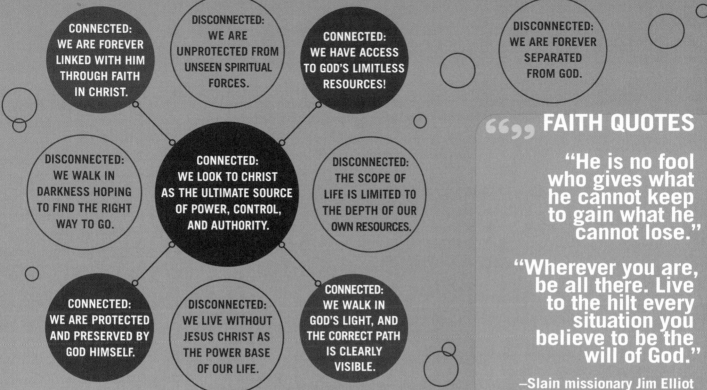

CONNECTED: WE ARE FOREVER LINKED WITH HIM THROUGH FAITH IN CHRIST.

DISCONNECTED: WE ARE UNPROTECTED FROM UNSEEN SPIRITUAL FORCES.

CONNECTED: WE HAVE ACCESS TO GOD'S LIMITLESS RESOURCES!

DISCONNECTED: WE ARE FOREVER SEPARATED FROM GOD.

DISCONNECTED: WE WALK IN DARKNESS HOPING TO FIND THE RIGHT WAY TO GO.

CONNECTED: WE LOOK TO CHRIST AS THE ULTIMATE SOURCE OF POWER, CONTROL, AND AUTHORITY.

DISCONNECTED: THE SCOPE OF LIFE IS LIMITED TO THE DEPTH OF OUR OWN RESOURCES.

CONNECTED: WE ARE PROTECTED AND PRESERVED BY GOD HIMSELF.

DISCONNECTED: WE LIVE WITHOUT JESUS CHRIST AS THE POWER BASE OF OUR LIFE.

CONNECTED: WE WALK IN GOD'S LIGHT, AND THE CORRECT PATH IS CLEARLY VISIBLE.

" FAITH QUOTES

"He is no fool who gives what he cannot keep to gain what he cannot lose."

"Wherever you are, be all there. Live to the hilt every situation you believe to be the will of God."

—Slain missionary Jim Elliot

FAITH QUOTES "

"So you see, faith by itself isn't enough. Unless it produces good deeds, it is dead and useless. Now someone may argue, 'Some people have faith; others have good deeds.' But I say, 'How can you show me your faith if you don't have good deeds?' I will show you my faith by my good deeds."

—James 2:17-18

WAITING HAS ITS BENEFITS

We prefer green lights to red lights because green means we can go. But in the Christian life there are a great many red lights. There are times when we have to wait. But many times the wait is God's way of telling us we need to know something more before we can continue further.

HERE ARE SOME SCRIPTURES THAT CAN HELP US FIND PURPOSE IN THE WAITING:

PSALM 62:5— OUR HOPE COMES FROM GOD.

PSALM 40:1— HE HEARS US WHEN WE PRAY.

ISAIAH 40:31— OUR STRENGTH IS RENEWED.

ISAIAH 64:4— WE WILL RECEIVE INCREDIBLE THINGS FROM GOD.

"Let us not lose heart in doing good, for in due time we will reap if we do not grow weary." (Galatians 6:9, NASB)

WAYS TO PUT YOUR FAITH INTO ACTION

VOLUNTEER
to help teach a children's Sunday school class at your church.

GO
on a short-term mission project.

VOLUNTEER
for a local homeless shelter or soup kitchen on a regular basis.

PROACTIVELY PURSUE
opportunities to help those who are poor, homeless, or in trouble.

LEAD
a Bible study for people your age out of your home.

DID YOU KNOW?

FAITH BY NUMBERS

9% of 18- to 34-year-olds believe the Bible is relevant to their lives.

53% of this age group reads the Bible less than once a year, or never.

80% say that their faith is very important, but only 34% say they are absolutely committed to Christianity.

(*Sources: Studies by Zondervan/ Harris Interactive and Barna Research Group quoted in* USA Today.)

TOP 10 SIGNS YOU MIGHT BE "RELIGOUS"

1. You've ever gone to Sunday school just so you could join the church softball team.

2. Your keychain is a rosary.

3. You think premarital sex could lead to dancing.

4. The W.W.J.D. on your flask stands for *What Would Jesus Drink?*

5. You've read all the Left Behind books—just to cover your bases.

6. Your lottery picks are the numbers from your favorite Scripture verses.

7. You wear a Christian T-shirt when out drinking with your friends—because it makes it less sinful.

8. You've attended Ash Wednesday mass for ten years and still don't know why the priest puts ashes on your forehead.

9. You've switched churches because someone sat in your seat one Sunday morning.

10. You've ever bummed a cigarette off of a deacon.

YOU'VE READ ALL THE LEFT BEHIND BOOKS

Q&A ABOUT Spiritual GIFTS

Q: DO SPIRITUAL GIFTS REALLY EXIST?

A: Yes, they do exist. Here's a quick explanation. When you become a follower of Jesus Christ, the Holy Spirit comes into your life and gives you spiritual talents (Romans 12:6). And God expects you to use those talents for the good of his Kingdom here on earth. It's your job to be ready and willing to be used.

Q: HOW AM I SUPPOSED TO KNOW WHAT MY SPIRITUAL GIFTS ARE?

A: Some well-known Christian authors and theologians suggest that your spiritual gifts are the talents that come naturally to you as a person. For instance, if you're a good singer and play a mean guitar, leading a crowd in praise and worship music might be your spiritual gift. Spiritual gifts listed in the Bible include serving, teaching, encouraging, and giving (Romans 12:6-9). If you're not exactly sure what you're called to do, there are online resources that can help you pinpoint what your specific gifts might be. Go ahead and Google "spiritual gifts test" and you will no doubt find one that is right for you!

Q: HOW DO I GO ABOUT USING MY SPIRITUAL GIFTS?

A: Your spiritual gifts can be used in many different ways. If your gift is teaching, then God might want you to lead a Bible study for teenagers or a children's Sunday school class. If your gift is leading praise and worship music, then look for opportunities to serve him through music, drama, and other forms of worship. Above all, resist the temptation to just sit back and do nothing. Your gifts could make a difference in someone's life, enrich your local church, or lead an entire generation closer to God!

MONEY—AN INTRODUCTION

IT'S ALL ABOUT THE BENJAMINS. OR AT LEAST THAT'S HOW IT SEEMS SOMETIMES. MONEY HAS A WAY OF SHAPING AND DRIVING YOU. WHAT DOES MONEY BUY FOR YOU? WE'RE NOT TALKING ABOUT A PIMPED-OUT RIDE OR THE LATEST KNOCKOFF LOUIS VUITTON HANDBAG. . . . WHAT IS IT THAT MONEY *REALLY* BUYS FOR YOU? SECURITY? SELF-WORTH? COMFORT? EMPOWERMENT? CONFIDENCE? MONEY MEANS SOMETHING DIFFERENT TO EVERYONE. THE DANGER IS THAT IF LEFT UNCHECKED, THE WEIGHT MONEY HAS IN YOUR LIFE MAY SLOW YOU DOWN OR PREVENT YOU FROM DOING WHAT GOD HAS CALLED YOU TO DO. THE BIBLE MAKES IT CLEAR THAT MONEY NEEDS TO BE HANDLED WITH CARE. ECCLESIASTES 5:10 OBSERVES, "THE ONE WHO LOVES MONEY IS NEVER SATISFIED WITH MONEY, NOR THE ONE WHO LOVES WEALTH WITH BIG PROFITS" *(THE MESSAGE)*. AND AS WARREN BUFFETT, THE CEO OF BERKSHIRE HATHAWAY, INC., NOTED, "IF YOU WERE A JERK BEFORE, YOU'LL BE A BIGGER JERK WITH A BILLION DOLLARS." YET IF USED WISELY, MONEY HAS THE ABILITY TO BLESS, ENCOURAGE, INSTILL HOPE, AND MAKE A DIFFERENCE IN COUNTLESS PEOPLE'S LIVES. IT CAN BE USED TO FEED THE HUNGRY, CLOTHE THE POOR, AND PUT A ROOF OVER PEOPLE'S HEADS. MONEY CAN ENABLE YOUNG PEOPLE TO PURSUE THEIR DREAMS AND OLD PEOPLE TO LIVE IN DIGNITY. MONEY OPENS UP OPPORTUNITIES FOR US TO GROW—TO LEARN VALUES, SELF-DISCIPLINE, AND GENEROSITY. BUT EVEN FOR ALL ITS BENEFITS, ULTIMATELY MONEY IS JUST PAPER AND COIN. A STRONG REMINDER OF THAT CAME ON JANUARY 1, 2002, WHEN A DOZEN EUROPEAN NATIONS BEGAN MAKING THE SWITCH FROM THEIR NATIONAL CURRENCIES TO THE NEW EURO. CITIZENS WERE GIVEN A GRACE PERIOD, AFTER WHICH ALL THE TRADITIONAL CURRENCIES, INCLUDING THE LIRA, FRANC, AND MARK, BECAME WORTHLESS. AN ARTICLE IN THE *CHICAGO TRIBUNE* REPORTED THAT PEOPLE GOT PRETTY CREATIVE ABOUT GETTING RID OF ALL THOSE LEFTOVER, WORTHLESS FUNDS. ONE STATE GOVERNMENT PLANNED TO BURN ITS CURRENCY IN ITS HEATING SYSTEM. A CARNIVAL IN GERMANY PLANNED TO USE THE NOTES AS CONFETTI. THE AUSTRIAN GOVERNMENT DECIDED TO TURN ITS SCHILLINGS INTO 560 TONS OF COMPOST. AND TWO RATHER MEMORABLE MEN DECIDED TO FILL AN EMPTY SWIMMING POOL WITH NEARLY $5 MILLION WORTH OF DEUTSCHE MARKS AND INVITE PEOPLE FOR A SWIM. NOW THAT'S A COOL PARTY! AS MUCH AS IT CAN BUY, AS MUCH POWER AS IT HOLDS, IT'S STILL JUST MONEY. THE POSSIBLE COMPOST FODDER OR SWIMMING-POOL FILLER OF THE FUTURE. THAT REALITY CHECK OPENS THE DOOR TO FREEDOM. FREEDOM TO HOLD THE THINGS OF THIS WORLD LOOSELY, REMEMBERING THAT THERE'S A GREATER WORLD TO COME. THERE'S A LOT TO LEARN ABOUT MONEY IN YOUR TWENTYS. ODDS ARE YOU HAVE A BOATLOAD OF STUDENT LOANS THAT NEED TO BE PAID BACK, AND EVEN IF YOU DON'T, THERE IS STILL A LOT TO LEARN ABOUT BASIC FINANCES, INCLUDING SAVING, INVESTING, DEBT MANAGEMENT, GOOD DEBT VERSUS BAD DEBT, GIVING, THE ROTH IRA AND 401(K), CREDIT REPORTS, IDENTITY THEFT, SOCIAL SECURITY, BALANCING A CHECKBOOK, AND OF COURSE, LEARNING HOW TO BE A SAVVY SHOPPER, WHICH IS PROBABLY THE MOST FUN. THE FUNNY THING ABOUT FINANCES IS THAT THE MORE YOU LEARN, THE MORE YOU DISCOVER THERE IS TO LEARN. CALCULATING INTEREST RATES, FUTURE INVESTMENTS, THE POTENTIAL OF STOCKS—IT CAN ALL BECOME PRETTY TIME-CONSUMING, AND EVEN PRETTY *LIFE*-CONSUMING. MONEY CAN'T BUY EVERYTHING—JUST TAKE A GOOD LOOK AT DONALD TRUMP'S HAIR—BUT IT WILL AFFECT YOUR TWENTYS AND BEYOND. SO AS YOU REFLECT ON MONEY AND WHAT YOU WANT IT TO DO (OR NOT DO) IN THE YEARS TO COME, REMEMBER THAT DECISIONS YOU MAKE NOW WILL EVENTUALLY SHAPE WHO YOU BECOME. AND THAT IS SOMETHING MONEY CAN'T BUY.

MONEY $

SINGING THE CHECKBOOK BLUES

Definition: Balancing Your Checkbook = Reconciling your checks and deposits; doing the basic math required to ensure that your balance matches the bank's balance.

THREE EASY WAYS TO RUIN YOUR CHECKBOOK BALANCE

① WRITE CHECKS LIKE YOU'RE WRITING THE FOLLOW-UP TO GRISHAM'S LATEST NOVEL, but don't record them in your checkbook.

② DUMP YOUR MONTHLY STATEMENTS FROM THE BANK LIKE YOU DID YOUR LAST DATE! Don't keep track of 'em and cut all ties.

③ USE MULTIPLE CHECKING ACCOUNTS AT ONCE. You won't know what's coming or going!

THREE EASY WAYS TO SALVAGE YOUR CHECKBOOK BALANCE

① USE YOUR CHECK REGISTER (that cute little paper ledger that came free with your checks) to record the details of each check you write. Write down the check number, date, description of transaction, and payment/debit or deposit/credit.

② IMMEDIATELY SUBTRACT THE CHECK AMOUNT OR ADD THE DEPOSIT AMOUNT TO REGISTER YOUR BALANCE. If you're not naturally good with numbers, pull out a calculator. Don't worry. You won't have to use any of the buttons with strange squiggles on them.

③ WHEN YOU RECEIVE YOUR MONTHLY STATEMENT FROM YOUR BANK, CHECK OFF EACH PAYMENT/DEBIT, DEPOSIT/CREDIT, AND FEE TO MAKE SURE ALL THE TOTALS MATCH. If there's a discrepancy, determine who made the error. If it's a personal error, make the correction in the ledger. If it's a bank error (and they happen more often than you realize), call the bank and have it corrected. Remember that you can't assume that the bank's statement is correct. You have to watch your own back on this one.

Get in the habit of balancing your checkbook once a month. The longer you wait, the harder it is to catch up, and you just may end up bouncing a check if you're not careful. So get ahead of the game and balance your checkbook today!

> **"GET IN THE HABIT OF BALANCING YOUR CHECKBOOK ONCE A MONTH."**

FIRST COMES EDUCATION, AND THEN COMES DEBT. For many graduates, the interest-bearing clock begins ticking on student loans shortly after they accept their diploma. So if you find yourself becoming best buddies with the likes of Fannie Mae, Freddie Mac, Mr. Perkins, Mrs. Stafford, or any other forms of student loan debt, it's important to begin tackling the debt right away.

When you signed up for your student loan, you may not have understood the full responsibility that came with it, but shortly after graduation you will begin to feel the full effect. Student loans require you to pay a combination of principal and interest until the loan is paid in full. Every loan is different—requiring different interest percentages and payback schedules. In some cases, repayment can be deferred for service in the armed forces or physical disability. And some loans allow you to reduce or even cancel the loan principal for serving in law enforcement or working with low-income or handicapped children. Needless to say, it's important to read all information from your loan program carefully. If you're unclear on any of the details, don't hesitate to call the company and ask for more information.

Because you've been collecting student loans for four years (or longer) without paying interest, you may think that the financial institutions behind the loans are lax when it comes to being paid back. Think again. Any defaulting on a student loan can tarnish your credit record for years to come. Even if you declare bankruptcy (which we don't recommend), student loans don't disappear. It's like belly button lint—it just won't go away.

The good news about student loans is that you can pay them off early and avoid countless years of frivolous interest. Simply by doubling up on your loan payments, you can cut your paid-in-full date dramatically. If you are disciplined enough to send in triple payments, you will be able to see the debt erased even faster. Your student loans may seem really big, but that doesn't mean you have to live with them forever. Focus on paying them off as quickly as possible—just as you would any other loan.

SAVING FOR A RAINY DAY?

Saving money is no longer a very popular idea for most Americans. In 1993, the average American was saving a measly 5.9 percent of disposable income. Ten years later, the same American was saving only 1.3 percent.

(Source: Bureau of Economic Analysis)

GOOD DEBT IS OKAY, BUT NO DEBT
IS ALWAYS BETTER

GOOD DEBT. Does it sound like an oxymoron? Maybe so, but *good debt* refers to debt that increases your ability to earn money and enhances your overall quality of life. Examples of good debt include a home mortgage or student loan, both of which enjoy lower interest rates than credit card debt. Student loans signify an investment in your earning potential over the course of a lifetime, and buying a home can be a healthy investment that appreciates for years to come. Classic examples of bad debt include credit cards and short-term, high-interest loans. Bad debts may give you the bling-bling in the short-term, but in the long-term, they'll cost you more than you ever expected.

Good debt is a lot like low-fat food. It's generally healthier than the full-fat alternatives, but too much of any good thing will weigh you down. In the end, good debt is still debt, and it needs to be paid back on time if not ahead of time. It's a step up from bad debt, which usually reduces your net worth and overall quality of life.

Your goal should be to live debt free. That means paying off your debts, often from the smallest to the largest. When you reach ground zero, you've hit a milestone, a landmark, a gold mine. You're finally able to save on interest, late fees, and excessive service charges. You can begin to save for things before you buy them. You can actually use credit cards for your benefit rather than the credit card company's advantage. And you're one step closer to smiling at the clerk and saying, "I'll be paying cash" on a large-ticket item. When you're debt free and aggressively saving, a dream trip to Europe, "tricking out" your ride, or saving for a down payment on a house are no longer out of reach—they're reality.

When you're debt free, you're free to begin saving money for life's emergencies, too. You can afford to put three to six months' savings in an account in case you're laid off or lose your job. Always remember that reaching zero debt isn't the end—it's the wonderful beginning to real financial freedom.

CAN WEALTH BUY HAPPINESS?

According to a recent article in the *Wall Street Journal*, almost 150 studies have shown that money can't buy happiness. Instead, happiness comes from enjoyable work, social relationships, a sense that life has meaning, and joining civic and other groups.

DID YOU KNOW?

NEED SOME QUICK
CASH?

Need some money fast? Skip the loan shark and cash in on these ideas:

HOLD A GARAGE SALE. Dump your unwanted items on those less discerning.

POST IT ON EBAY. People will buy anything these days—really.

PUT IT IN THE PAPER. Have something worth more than two hundred dollars that you're willing to part with? You can cash in quick with an ad in tomorrow's paper.

USE YOUR SKILLS. Know how to do an oil change? Sell your services to your friends for cheap, as long as you can make a profit.

HOUSE-SIT OR DOG-SIT. Know someone going out of town? Offer to care for their animals or house. Just be clear about what you charge before you agree to take care of anyone's "pet" alligator.

LIVIN' LIKE A PAUPER, WANTING TO BE A PRINCE (OR PRINCESS)

It's easy to think you can move out of your parents' home and right into one just like it (or even nicer) right now in your twentys. And the temptation with all those credit card offers and low-interest loans is to live above, sometimes far above, what you actually earn. But the reality is that your parents worked several decades to get where they are financially today, and if you want to get there responsibly, there's a good chance it's going to take you a few decades too.

Your parents may have returned to DINK status (Double Income, No Kids). They may have most of their home paid off. They may be able to afford nice vacations or drive new cars. Mom may go on shopping sprees while Dad buys the latest gadget or gizmo. All the while, you're looking at your ten-dollars-an-hour job wondering how you're going to make your next student loan payment. So how do you stay happy living on Top Ramen while they're eating prime rib?

First, remember that your parents faced the same hardships and challenges after graduation that you face today. It took them years of saving and sacrifice to be able to afford the luxuries they're enjoying now. And eventually, things do (hopefully) get easier. Promotions happen. Pay increases finally arrive. And with enough wise investing and financial planning, you can get ahead—sometimes even far ahead. So don't let Mom and Dad or that dorky guy from high school who went public with his little online business in early 2000 and hit it big throw you off. You're doing just fine. Really.

YOU HAVE TO $AVE MORE THAN YOU $PEND

IT'S NO SECRET IN THE WORLD OF DIETING that you have to burn more calories than you consume if you're going to lose weight. It's no different when it comes to finances. You have to save more than you spend if you're going to get ahead. Unfortunately, between the checkbook, debit card, good old-fashioned cash, and all those credit cards, it's easy to lose track of what you're spending. So the first step in getting a handle on your finances is figuring out where all your money is going.

You don't have to be Suze Orman to understand finances. In fact, you can do it in less than thirty days. Just spend one month getting the 4-1-1 on your expenses and purchases. Collect your receipts in a shoe box, envelope, or that cool bag you got the last time you were shopping. Or if you're disciplined and can pay off the monthly balance, you can make all your purchases on a credit card and use the statement at the end of month to track your expenditures.

In a small notebook or journal, list your fixed expenses (rent, utilities, car payments, auto insurance, and student loan payments). On the second page, make a list of other not-so-necessary expenditures (entertainment, groceries, gym membership, a trip to Tuscany, the latest Naked Chef cookbook—because you really thought he was in his birthday suit—and latest additions to your bobblehead collection). Add up all of your expenditures and compare the total to your income. Which is greater?

If you're spending more than you're making, then you need to either cut your expenses (aka, cut your cable bill and watch Jon Stewart at your friend's house) or look for a second job. The fact is that if you don't make a change, you're going to sink deeper into debt. The deeper you go, the harder it is to get back out, which means there's no time better than the present to make some changes.

On the other hand, if you're making more than you're spending, then congratulations—you're on the right track. But once you're done patting yourself on the back, take a moment and challenge yourself to find where you could save even more. By taking a hard look at your expenses, you may find areas that you can cut back and discover "new money" to pay off student loans early or save for a down payment on a house. Or you may discover that by tightening your belt you can afford to contribute more to your 401(k), give more money to your favorite charity, or pay back any other debts.

So instead of maxing out your credit cards with spending, try to max out your 401(k), IRA, and bank account with saving. You'll find that life is a lot more comfortable and less stressful in the black than it is in the red. With the weight of debt off your back, you'll be free to fly.

① Buy your food at less trendy grocery stores. Remember that you pay extra for all the amenities.

② Fast (you know, as in the biblical sense of the word).

③ Take advantage of promos, discounts, and two-for-ones at local restaurants.

9
WAYS
TO CUT
YOUR FOOD BUDGET

④ Shop with a friend and buy in bulk. Then split the jumbo cost and goods.

⑤ Double coupons, anyone?

⑥ Keep your recipes simple. Exotic ingredients add up quick.

⑦ Remember that making it from scratch can get pricey. A onetime batch of cookies from scratch can cost more than ten dollars if you have to buy all the ingredients, whereas a bag of cookies or a tube of dough can go for under three dollars.

⑧ Gnaw on your hand.

⑨ Drink water. It's fat free, sugar free, cholesterol free, sodium free, and even flavor free—not to mention that it's usually cost free. What more could you want?

ACCIDENTS HAPPEN
& YOU'D BETTER BE INSURED

INSURANCE CAN GET PRETTY EXPENSIVE. Car insurance, renter's insurance, health insurance, and life insurance are just the beginning. Some companies are willing to insure anything—use your imagination—for a price. If you stop by a local insurance office, you'll discover that just about anything and everything can (and in their opinion should) be insured. It can all seem a bit overwhelming not only to you but also to your bottom line. TwentysOnline.com provides valuable information about buying or reviewing insurance policies and offers competitive insurance policies for people in their twentys.

But where should you begin right now? With the basics. Here's some information to help you:

CAR INSURANCE *So you wanna "trick out" your ride?* State laws require car owners to have a basic policy, which usually includes liability. Depending on the year and value of your car, you may want to upgrade your policy. But if you're driving a clunker, you could opt for a higher deductible and skip some of the bells and whistles they'll try to sell you. Many online sites offer quick estimates of where to trim or expand coverage. Investigate the rates before you buy your next car. You may be surprised how insurance varies depending on the particular model and year you have in mind.

RENTER'S INSURANCE *So you wanna protect your crib?* For a few hundred dollars, you can have your goods replaced if your forgetful neighbor torches the place by leaving the barbecue on all night.

HEALTH INSURANCE *So you wanna protect yourself?* If you can still qualify under your parents' policy, ride the coattails of their insurance carrier for as long as possible. Once you're on your own, things get a bit tricky. If your place of employment offers insurance, sign up right away. If you're self-employed or unemployed, then you should still opt for a major medical care policy (if you can't afford a standard policy) in case something happens. With a week in the hospital running as much as fifty thousand dollars, you can't afford not to be insured.

DID YOU KNOW?

INSURANCE TIP

When calculating your insurance rates, insurers often estimate your age from your nearest birthday—which means they may consider you a year older than you actually are, and that could cost you more money. Lock in lower premiums by purchasing insurance within the first six months of your birthday.

LIFE INSURANCE *So you wanna live forever?* It may seem a little early—after all, you're still in your prime—but this is when you can lock in the best life insurance rates. So consult with a local agency to see what coverage is available. You may find you're able to afford more than you thought—and down the road you'll be glad you locked into a good rate early. Just be sure you get all the facts before signing on the dotted line!

While you can trust insurance to provide coverage for big-ticket items, there are a number of smaller-ticket items that can catch you by surprise. The mechanic quotes you a $1,200 price to fix your car engine. A flood in your apartment ruins your furniture and clothes. Your hard drive calls it quits. You get two flat tires. You need to buy a plane ticket home unexpectedly. You're asked to be in three weddings this year, and you have no idea how you're going to afford it all. Life can get expensive fast. That's why it's important to have an emergency fund. In a perfect world, you'd sock away about six months' income into a rainy day just-in-case-you-get-laid-off-or-have-a-major-accident account. But even if you can't save a whopping six months' income, you can still start an account with $300, $500, or $1,000 to help you in time of need. It may seem hard to do now, but we guarantee you won't regret it later. So start your own private insurance policy because—let's face it—life happens. • • • • • • • • •

CREDIT CARD COMPANIES LIKE TO GO
· · · · · · · · · · · · · · · ·*BLING-BLING*

In case you haven't noticed, credit card companies are doing all they can to make you feel comfortable with debt. They don't want you to see *d-e-b-t* as a four-letter word, so they're using all kinds of incentives—everything from points and miles programs to rebates—to entice you to use your credit card rather than a debit card, check, or cash. Why? Because they make money not only on every transaction but also on the interest from your late payments.

In fact, credit card companies would love for you to put all of your living expenses—including utilities, groceries, gym memberships, and other monthly bills—on your credit card. One of the latest additions to the list of charge-'ems is taxes. That's right. The Internal Revenue Service will allow you to pay a portion or all of your taxes with your credit card (as long as you pay a fee, of course).

What's with the big-market push toward credit cards? A decade ago, you couldn't use your MasterCard/Visa/American Express/Discover at your local drive-thru. But slowly the use of plastic is becoming standard even in the fast-food industry. Studies show that when a person pays with plastic, they spend 25 to 30 percent more when they're shopping.

So the bottom line is that credit card companies want you to be as comfy with your credit card as you are in a La-Z-Boy recliner. Resist the urge to kick back and zone out. Watch your debt, and if it's getting the best of you, cut up the cards and shift to cash, checks, or debit—where you'll be less tempted to spend more than you have to.

DID YOU KNOW?

PLASTIC, PLEASE

The average American has eight—yep, that's right, *eight*—credit cards.

POOR AFRICA

The five poorest countries of the world according to WorldAtlas.com are Congo, Ethiopia, Eritrea, Somalia, and Mozambique.

And don't forget to check the latest agreement on your current credit cards. When you signed up with your current cards, you might have landed an introductory deal promising 4.6 percent or even 0 percent interest and no late fees. But odds are that offer has expired and your interest charges may have quadrupled overnight. So check out the new terms, and if they don't look good, transfer your balance onto a new card with better terms. Always remember that you don't have to let your credit cards get the best of you.

A ZERO BALANCE. PRICELESS.

MAKE A DENT IN YOUR CAR INSURANCE

LOOKING FOR WAYS TO CUT BACK ON YOUR AUTO INSURANCE? HERE ARE A FEW TIPS:

1. ADD UP THE DISCOUNTS WITH ANTILOCK BRAKES, ANTI-THEFT DEVICES, AND LOW MILEAGE.

2. DRIVE WITH A CLEAN RECORD. IF YOU CAN CLOCK THREE YEARS WITHOUT AN ACCIDENT OR TICKET, YOU CAN QUALIFY FOR THE LOWEST PREMIUMS.

3. COMPARE PRICES AT DIFFERENT CARRIERS.

4. IF YOU DRIVE AN OLDER VEHICLE, CONSIDER DROPPING COLLISION AND/OR COMPREHENSIVE INSURANCE, OR AT LEAST RAISE THE DEDUCTIBLE TO A THOUSAND DOLLARS.

5. REVIEW YOUR CREDIT SCORE. YOU MAY BE SURPRISED TO FIND THERE'S A LINK BETWEEN YOUR CREDIT SCORE AND YOUR INSURANCE SCORE—A FIGURE THAT INSURERS OFTEN USE TO SET RATES.

6. CHECK OUT PRICES ONLINE AT WWW.TWENTYSONLINE.COM.

7. SELL YOUR CAR AND BUY A BIKE.

Making the Grade
ON YOUR CREDIT REPORT

A+

A credit report is a lot like a report card, except that it doesn't just follow you around for four years—it tracks you for life. A credit report lists your full name, contact information, Social Security number, age, and employment history. It also includes your monthly payment history with all creditors from mortgage companies to credit card companies, court records of any tax liens or bankruptcies, as well as a list of anyone who has requested access to your report in the past one to two years.

A credit score ranging from 300 to 800 provides a snapshot of your creditworthiness. You may not think it's important now, but when you go to apply for another credit card, buy a car, or buy a home, it's going to be really important. So take time to make sure everything on your report is accurate. Check out www.equifax.com, www.experian.com, or www.transunion.com to buy a copy of your report. It's money well spent.

And what if you find that you score a big, fat F (let's say a score of 320) on your credit report? Well, don't lose hope. You can begin boosting your score by finding any inaccuracies and contacting the companies to make things right. If you have a bomber score, then you can raise it by making sure you start paying your bills on time. Pay back any pushy loan officers, and if possible, consolidate your debt into one easy payment you can afford. You'll be surprised how quickly your score will improve.

➤ THINK CREDIT CARDS ARE BAD?

Did you know that without a credit card . . .

↳ YOU'D HAVE TO WALK INTO THE GAS STATION TO PAY FOR YOUR GAS. OVER THE COURSE OF YOUR LIFE THAT WILL TAKE .04 YEARS OFF YOUR LIFE SPAN, ACCORDING TO AN UNOFFICIAL, UNSCIENTIFIC STUDY.

↳ YOU'D HAVE A HARD TIME STAYING AT A HOTEL BECAUSE THEY ALMOST ALWAYS REQUIRE A CREDIT CARD FOR A DAMAGE DEPOSIT.

↳ YOU COULD MISS OUT ON EARNING ZILLIONS OF AIRLINE MILES, POINTS, AND OTHER REBATES.

↳ YOU WON'T GET AN END-OF-THE-YEAR STATEMENT THAT SAYS WHERE ALL YOUR GREENBACKS WENT.

↳ YOU WILL HAVE A TOUGH TIME GETTING A LOAN. NO CREDIT HISTORY = NO LOAN.

↳ YOU'D LOOK FRUMPY FROM ALL THOSE DOLLARS AND COINS IN YOUR POCKETS.

See—credit cards aren't all that bad. But remember that you have to use them wisely . . . aka, pay them off every month.

TIPS FOR THE CHRONIC
SPENDER

Love to spend money? If so, you're not alone. Shopping.
Spending. Buying. It's all so fun. No wonder the devil
wears Prada. So how do you make sure your little shopping
habit doesn't get the best of you?

❶ Make a list of what you need before you ever leave
home. Stick to the list!

❷ Remember that just because it's on sale doesn't mean
you have to buy it. There will be more sales—guaranteed!

❸ Ask yourself, *Do I already own one of these?* If so, you
probably don't need another.

❹ Open a savings account that limits your withdrawals.
Don't let yourself tap into the account.

❺ Get in the habit of paying off your credit card bills every month.

If you can't kick the spending habit, then start using cash.
When your wallet is empty, you're done!

NAME-BRAND GOODS@
OFF-BRAND PRICES

Looking for a Gucci handbag, eight-hundred-thread count
Egyptian sheets, or Sergio Rossi boots? Then it's time
to go online for some of the best finds on the Web. At
www.bluefly.com and **www.designeroutlet.com**, you'll discover
big-name fashion at a fraction of the cost. Gotta love it!
If you're willing to venture into used clothing, visit
www.christabellescloset.com, where vintage name brands
abound. If you want the latest Krups coffeepot, head to
www.overstock.com, which is loaded with all types of household
products. And if you're looking for luxurious labels, go no
further than **www.netaporter.com**, where you'll find Jimmy
Choo and more!

How much money do you think you need for retirement? What's the number that comes to mind? Write it below:

Okay, now let's look at your number. If you retire at the age of fifty, let's say, a million dollars in the bank earning a modest 5 percent interest, you'll be able to live on fifty-thousand dollars a year without dipping into your savings (which is probably a good idea since you won't be able to collect Social Security for another fifteen years). Fifty-thousand dollars may seem like a lot at first glance, but don't forget that you still have to pay federal income tax and possibly state income tax on that money (depending on where you live). And you'll have health insurance and life insurance and auto insurance and all kinds of fixed costs, including property taxes, a mortgage, and living expenses. And you'll probably have children and college tuition and all kinds of expenses you never imagined.

Suddenly fifty thousand dollars, let alone a million dollars, doesn't seem like that much. Maybe two million would do. . . . Whatever number you're shooting for, it's important to remember that getting there is just as important as being there.

Retirement is taking on new meaning for the twentys generation. Retirement is no longer just about a condo in south Florida with plastic flamingos out front or another round of golf where you try your best not to say four-letter words—it's about doing something meaningful with the last years of your life. If you have a fulfilling career, you're naturally going to want a fulfilling retirement. You may want to save aggressively and retire early, or you may decide to work longer, pushing off retirement as long as possible.

Either way, you should try to save 15 percent of your gross annual income per year. Make some investments, too—some conservative and some more risky. And stay on top of your financial portfolio. But along the way, remember that the greatest investments you'll ever make are going to be in people's lives, not in mutual funds.

So do your homework, find a good stockbroker or investment counselor, and do everything you can to prepare financially for the future. But don't allow the rush to retire rob you of all that God wants you to invest into people along the way.

YOU MAY HAVE ACCESS TO FREE MONEY

Lots of companies offer matching funds—usually between 3 to 5 percent of your salary—for people who participate in a 401(k). Taking advantage of the offer is like accepting free money. So invest away!

DID YOU KNOW?

TOO MUCH MONEY?

Did you suddenly have a financial windfall? If so, here are off-the-wall ideas on what to do with all that extra cash:

WALLPAPER.

ASK THE BANK TO GIVE YOU ALL THE MONEY IN ONES. MAKE A BIG PILE AND DIVE INTO IT.

SEW THE BILLS TOGETHER FOR AN EXPENSIVE OUTFIT.

TUCK MONEY INTO THE POCKETS OF ALL YOUR WINTER AND SUMMER CLOTHING SO YOU CAN HAVE THAT "COOL—I JUST FOUND CASH" FEELING YEAR-ROUND.

USE SMALLER BILLS TO CREATE A PAPIER-MACHÉ MASTERPIECE.

PRACTICE YOUR ORIGAMI.

Q & A: THE ROTH IRA

WHAT IS AN IRA?
An IRA is an Individual Retirement Account that allows you to save several thousand dollars a year tax free. You don't have to pay taxes on contributions—which earn compound interest—only on the money you withdraw during retirement.

WHAT'S A ROTH IRA?
It's similar to an IRA, except that it allows your savings to grow tax free. You pay taxes on your contributions but not on your withdrawals.

WHY SHOULD I INVEST IN AN IRA?
Because it offers a huge tax advantage. Unlike your regular savings and investment accounts, all your contributions to an IRA grow and compound without current taxes, which over the years can drastically improve the size of your retirement savings.

WHO CAN INVEST IN A ROTH IRA?
Almost anyone. There are some limitations, but the average person can invest in a Roth IRA.

HOW MUCH CAN YOU INVEST IN A ROTH IRA?
The maximum is currently $4,000 per year, per person.

DO I HAVE TO PAY TAXES?
Yes—you have to pay taxes on the money before you invest in a Roth IRA, but you do not have to pay taxes on the profits earned when you take the money out.

IS THERE ANY WAY TO AVOID THE TAXES?
Yes—you can invest in a traditional IRA. You won't have to pay the taxes on the $4,000 investment, but when you retire, you'll have to pay the taxes on all of your profits.

HOW MUCH OF A DIFFERENCE CAN A ROTH IRA MAKE ON MY RETIREMENT?
If you invest a mere $3,000 into a Roth IRA at age thirty-five and invest that amount every year until you're sixty-five and earn 12 percent interest, you'll have $873,000 tax-free at age sixty-five. It's an impressive number when you realize that you invested only $90,000 (that's $3,000 for thirty years). That's the power of compound interest! If you begin investing even earlier than age thirty-five (which is highly recommended) then you'll be even further ahead financially when it's time to retire.

WHAT IF I NEED TO USE THE MONEY BEFORE I RETIRE?
A Roth IRA is more flexible than a traditional IRA, but it still has limitations. In other words, a Roth IRA will let you fly at a higher altitude, but you still can't go into orbit. One of the major advantages of a Roth IRA is that you can use the money if you're a first-time homebuyer to purchase your crib without getting a slap on the wrist (aka, a penalty) from Uncle Sam. You can also use the funds if you become disabled (something we hope doesn't happen to you). But otherwise, withdrawing your funds early (before you turn sixty) will result in a 10-percent penalty and income tax bills. Yikes! But the financial details are often based on the age of the account, the owner's age, and the time elapsed since contributions were last made—and a bunch of other financial jargon. Talk to an accountant to get the 4-1-1 on the current year's tax rules before making any withdrawals.

THE GIVER ALWAYS GETS

Shel Silverstein's best-selling children's book *The Giving Tree* tells the story of a boy and a tree. Each day the boy visits the tree to swing from its beautiful branches and eat its delicious apples. Both the tree and the boy are very happy. But as the years pass, the boy asks for more and more from the tree, and the tree gives and gives until at last the tree is nothing but a stump. This powerful story is open to a variety of interpretations about selfless giving, relentless taking, or even the joy and pain that come from giving until you can't give any more. But the bottom line is that there is an undeniable pleasure that comes from giving.

Just ask Ben Stein about his money. Okay, bad example. But still, you were created to be a blessing to others. The ways you give aren't limited to wrapped gifts or a handful of cash or a written check. Rather, giving involves all of you—your time, resources, and energy. At times, the greatest gift you can give is as simple as a listening ear, a patient response, or a warm embrace.

There's also a mysterious nature to giving in that as you give to others, you receive something intangibly wonderful in return. Sometimes it's joy or satisfaction. Sometimes it's a sense of obedience to God's little nudges. And sometimes the rewards aren't seen or experienced until this life has passed. Maybe that's one reason Jesus encourages us to give to "the least of these" (Matthew 25:40) and maybe that's why "God loves a person who gives cheerfully" (2 Corinthians 9:7).

When it comes to financial giving, you may actually be able to afford to give more if you get receipts for what you give. Most churches, charities, and even some nonprofit organizations can provide a receipt for both financial gifts and goods donated. If you keep track of your receipts, you can get a tax break every year—enabling you to give even more!

Why don't you consider sponsoring a child through Compassion International or supporting a missionary overseas in addition to your regular tithe to your local church?

If you want to do your homework before giving to a nonprofit organization, visit the Better Business Bureau's Wise Giving Alliance Web site at www.give.org to find out how the organization you're giving to handles its funds.

You may think that you can't afford to give right now, but give it a second thought. It's precisely when you can't afford to give that giving means the most—even if it's a small amount. Remember the widow who put her two mites into the offering (Luke 21:1-4)? No one really noticed except one person—Jesus. And he still notices those who give today.

HEY LADY, THAT'S NEGOTIABLE

Linda Babcock, coauthor of *Women Don't Ask: Negotiation and the Gender Divide*, discovered that in a study of Carnegie Mellon graduates with master's degrees, 57 percent of men negotiated their first salary while only 7 percent of women did the same. Men that bargained increased their salaries by 7.4 percent, to the tune of around $4,000 more a year! If you need help negotiating, check out this book!

DEALS   FLIGHTS   HOTELS   CARS   VACATIONS   TRAVEL

www.TwentysOnline.com

www.travelocity.com

www.expedia.com

www.orbitz.com

www.travelzoo.com

www.qixo.com

www.mobissimo.com

www.priceline.com

www.hotwire.com

www.hotels.com

www.lodging.com

www.onetravel.com

www.biddingfortravel.com

www.TwentysOnline.com

This is one of the only sources of travel deals specifically designed for twentys. This site offers everything from simple airline and rental-car booking to special weekend packages all over the world. This is a great place to find information and travel deals that fit the active (and frugal!) lifestyle of a twenty.

www.travelocity.com, www.expedia.com, www.orbitz.com

These are three of the other most popular online travel sites. These Web sites give you the best rates they can find for car rentals, flights, and hotels.

www.travelzoo.com

This site offers a free subscription to a weekly list of the top twenty travel deals from across the country. You'll find cut-rate deals on everything from flights to hotels to resort packages—and you'll be hard-pressed to find these deals anywhere else. If you don't want to subscribe, you can still visit the site for the latest listings and recent deals.

www.qixo.com

This site offers competitive prices on everything from cars and flights to hotels and cruises. Add it to your online travel search list.

www.mobissimo.com

Mobissimo searches all the other online sites to find the best prices and link you to whichever site—whether it's **www.hotels.com, www.lodging.com,** or **www.onetravel.com**—that will offer you the best deal.

www.priceline.com, www.hotwire.com

If you're flexible about your flight times and don't care about the name of your hotel or car-rental company, then you can save big bucks with these bidding sites. But before you place a bid, stop by **www.biddingfortravel.com**, which offers message boards full of the information you'll need to make an educated bid.

THE PAYOFF QUIZ //////////////////////////////////

QUESTION: You have the following three debts: $10,000 in student loans at 5% interest; $5,000 in hospital bills at 7% interest; and $1,000 on your credit card at 4% interest. Which one should you pay off first?

ANSWER: You might be tempted to pay off the $5,000 hospital bill first because it has the highest interest rate. That's a good idea if you're really disciplined. But if you're feeling overwhelmed by the total amount of debt, then you're better off paying off the $1,000 on your credit card first. Sure, the interest rate is lower, but it will serve as a morale booster to get it paid off. Once you have a zero balance, then begin applying your payment toward the next largest debt—the hospital bills. Then it's time to tackle those student loans. ● ● ●

Q & A ON SOCIAL SECURITY //////////

WHAT IS SOCIAL SECURITY ANYWAY?
Founded in 1935 by the U.S. government, Social Security is a basic retirement plan designed to cover most of the nation's workforce. It provides limited payments for retirees as well as those with disabilities. It also includes Medicare benefits.

WILL SOCIAL SECURITY BE AROUND WHEN IT'S TIME FOR ME TO RETIRE?
There's a good chance Social Security will be around—but it may not offer the same benefits or payout scale as it does today. Projected benefits are expected to decrease, and the age of eligibility is likely to increase.

CAN I RETIRE ON SOCIAL SECURITY?
Social Security isn't meant to be your retirement savings account. It's merely a small sliver of your retirement. For millions of elderly Americans, a few hundred dollars extra from Social Security each month helps pull them above the brink of poverty.

HOW DO I KNOW HOW MUCH SOCIAL SECURITY I QUALIFY FOR?
Check out www.socialsecurity.gov or call the Social Security Administration at 1-800-772-1213 and ask for Form 7004: "Request for a Social Security Statement." Fill out the form, and within six weeks you'll get a free estimate of your retirement benefits. Yeah, we like that word: *free*. Check the information—which includes a record of earnings—for errors. ● ● ●

DID YOU KNOW?

WHAT ARE THE ODDS?
The odds of the IRS bringing you into a face-to-face encounter with Uncle Sam are about one in six hundred. Phew!

A NEW YOU?
IDENTITY THEFT

Over the last five years, identity theft has become the number one cause of shopper complaints from credit card users. It's estimated that every seventy-nine seconds a thief steals someone's identity! To clear up the mess, the victim has to jump through hoops, filling out countless forms to make things right. And depending on the damage the identity thief does, it can get pretty stinkin' expensive. . . .

TO AVOID GETTING TAKEN—

• Sign all checks with a gel pen. That's the one type of ink that is counterfeit-proof to acetone or other chemicals thieves use to steal and recreate your checks.

• Buy a shredder. Even a twenty-dollar model will ensure that your financial receipts don't end up in the wrong hands.

• Don't give out your Social Security number (SSN) unless you know you're responding to a credible request. Avoid putting your SSN on any checks—offer a driver's license number instead.

• Avoid entering personal information on Internet sites that don't have secure pages.

You've established a budget. You've cut out excess expenditures. You've set your financial goal, and you've given up several double-tall lattes, two lunches at Bennigan's, and a really cool pair of Lucky jeans in the last month to make it happen. And it's finally happening! Your discipline, hard work, and good old-fashioned thrift are paying off. You're climbing out of debt and you're getting ahead.

It feels good. It should. But sooner or later, you're going to find that all that penny-pinching can get pretty old. So set up a plan to reward yourself along the way. Develop a fun-money account and enjoy a treat. Have a nice dinner with friends. Buy yourself a massage. Go away for the weekend. And remind yourself that all that saving really does pay off. • • • • • • • • • •

REWARDING YOURSELF
ALONG THE WAY

DID YOU KNOW?

BIGHEARTED GIFTS WITH SMALL PRICE TAGS

It seems like every time you turn around there's another birthday, wedding, or celebration. And who doesn't feel the financial pinch during the holidays? Here are a few quick gift ideas that won't break the bank:

HOMEMADE GIFTS—Brush up on some of your long-lost hobbies or develop a new one. Make stationery, gift cards, soap, candles, wood carvings, or paintings. Use your natural talent and some free time to create a personal gift for someone you love.

THE VIDEO TRIBUTE—Who wouldn't love to have a movie made about them? Dust off the video camera and interview friends and family members for a funny but endearing present.

SCRAPBOOKS—Do you have stacks of photos from the time you've spent with your loved ones? Turn them into a mini scrapbook or pick the best picture and frame it. The simple but personal gift will speak volumes.

PLAY CHEF FOR A DAY—Instead of buying a gift, create something delicious in the kitchen. Bake cookies, pastries, or an entire romantic meal for two.

SIX REASONS TO SHOP AT
THE DOLLAR STORE

You've seen them all over. Tucked into strip malls. Nestled a few doors down from Wal-Mart. There's probably one in your local mall. It's the dollar store, where everything really is just a dollar (except the items that are two, three, or four for a dollar). They have different names. There's the Dollar Tree, Dollar General, Family Dollar, and Fred's. Some of the stuff is junky, like the one-eyed glass mermaid figurine made in China. Some of the stuff is cheap, like the kids' board book, which would make a great gift for your niece. And some of the stuff is too good to be true, like the name-brand cleaner that would have cost you four times as much at the local grocery store. Despite the cool deals, we don't recommend that guys buy their girlfriends' engagement rings there. Sometimes you just need to go for quality, you know?

SO HERE ARE SIX REASONS TO ADD THE DOLLAR STORE TO YOUR SHOPPING EXPERIENCE:

1. **YOU CAN FINALLY GET RID OF ALL THAT SPARE CHANGE.**

2. **YOU CAN FIND THE PERFECT PORCELAIN DUST COLLECTOR FOR GRANDMA.**

3. **YOU CAN GO ON A SHOPPING BINGE AND STILL SPEND LESS THAN TWENTY BUCKS.**

4. **YOU JUST MIGHT FIND A GREAT COSTUME FOR HALLOWEEN.**

5. **YOU'RE HUNGRY FOR A CHEAP SNACK.**

6. **YOU'RE BOUND TO DISCOVER AT LEAST THREE THINGS YOU DIDN'T KNOW YOU COULDN'T LIVE WITHOUT.**

EVERYTHING REALLY IS JUST A DOLLAR

9 THINGS TO DO WITH ALL THAT CHANGE

1. Give it to the next homeless guy you see. Make his day.

2. Buy ice cream cones for your coworkers.

3. Pick out the quarters and do your laundry.

4. Buy a needy kid a gift.

5. Take a friend to the arcade for an afternoon.

6. Pay for the car behind you the next time you drive through a tollbooth.

7. Take it to the bank and discover how change really does add up.

8. Surprise yourself by stuffing the pockets of a coat you won't wear until next year.

9. Buy flowers for your mom or someone else who has invested in you.

DID YOU KNOW?
SPOT BUDGETING

Can't keep up with a monthly budget? Then try spot budgeting. Simply identify two or three areas where you think you can cut back, and concentrate on those. Focus on insurance or groceries or entertainment or travel, rather than on every category at once.

Six Steps to Easy Budgeting

① SAVE ALL RECEIPTS FOR A MONTH.

② DIVIDE RECEIPTS INTO CATEGORIES SUCH AS RENT, UTILITIES, FOOD, ENTERTAINMENT, ETC.

③ COMPARE TOTAL MONTHLY EXPENSES TO TOTAL MONTHLY INCOME.

④ IF EXPENSES ARE GREATER THAN INCOME, LOOK FOR WAYS TO CUT BACK.

⑤ IF INCOME IS GREATER THAN EXPENSES, LOOK FOR WAYS TO INVEST.

⑥ REPEAT THE PROCEDURE FOR A SECOND MONTH AND IMPLEMENT ANY NECESSARY CHANGES.

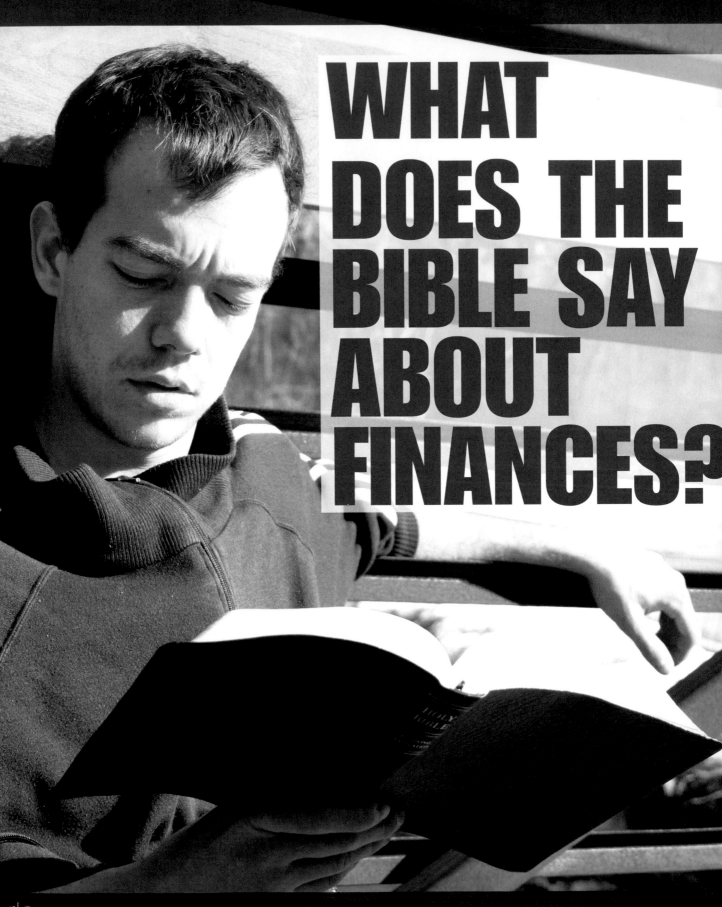

WHAT DOES THE BIBLE SAY ABOUT FINANCES?

THERE ARE A LOT OF FINANCIAL ADVISORS, many of whom offer good ideas on how to manage your money. But the Bible has a lot to say about finances too. Take a few moments to reflect on the following verses. In what ways do they confirm your attitudes and handling of money? In what ways do they challenge you to make some personal changes?

"A good name is more desirable than great riches; to be esteemed is better than silver or gold." —PROVERBS 22:1, NIV

"Whoever trusts in his riches will fall, but the righteous will thrive like a green leaf."—PROVERBS 11:28, NIV

"The wicked borrow and never repay, but the godly are generous givers." —PSALM 37:21

"A man who makes a vow to the Lord or makes a pledge under oath must never break it. He must do exactly what he said he would do."—NUMBERS 30:2

"Owe nothing to anyone—except for your obligation to love one another. If you love your neighbor, you will fulfill the requirements of God's law."—Romans 13:8

"The borrower becomes the lender's slave." —PROVERBS 22:7, NASB

"You will be made rich in every way so that you can be generous on every occasion, and through us your generosity will result in thanksgiving to God."
—2 CORINTHIANS 9:11, NIV

"A generous man will prosper; he who refreshes others will himself be refreshed."—PROVERBS 11:25, NIV

"Be careful that no one entices you by riches; do not let a large bribe turn you aside."—JOB 36:18, NIV

"O God, I beg two favors from you; let me have them before I die. First, help me never to tell a lie. Second, give me neither poverty nor riches! Give me just enough to satisfy my needs. For if I grow rich, I may deny you and say, 'Who is the Lord?' And if I am too poor, I may steal and thus insult God's holy name."
—PROVERBS 30:7-9

CULTURE—AN INTRODUCTION

A YOUNG MAN FROM FAIRFAX, VIRGINIA, LEAVES THE COMFORT OF HIS LARGE, PLUSH HOUSE, HIS $80,000-A-YEAR JOB, AND THE LOVE AND SUPPORT OF HIS COMMUNITY AND CROSSES THE OCEAN TO BECOME A FULL-TIME MISSIONARY ON THE SHORELINES OF NORWAY. WHEN HE GETS THERE, HE REALIZES THAT MUCH OF WHAT HE HAS LEARNED ABOUT MINISTRY IN THE STATES DOESN'T TRANSLATE TO LIFE IN NORWAY, SO HE EXCITEDLY BEGINS LEARNING HOW TO REACH OUT TO A WHOLE NEW CULTURE. A TWENTY-THREE-YEAR-OLD GIRL SPENDS FIVE YEARS STUDYING ART AND THE HISTORY OF FILMMAKING IN COLLEGE. AFTER GRADUATING, SHE MOVES TO LOS ANGELES TO PURSUE A CAREER PRODUCING AND DIRECTING MOVIES—A DREAM SHE HAS HAD SINCE SHE WAS A TEENAGER. BUT ONLY DAYS AFTER SHE ARRIVES, HER PURSE IS STOLEN, SHE GETS A BIG FAT NO FROM A JOB PROSPECT, AND HER PARENTS CALL TO SAY THEY THINK SHE SHOULD MOVE BACK TO NEBRASKA. SHE REFUSES. A TWENTY-NINE-YEAR-OLD BANKER FROM CHARLESTON, SOUTH CAROLINA, SITS AT HOME WITH HIS WIFE ALMOST EVERY NIGHT WATCHING DVDS, LISTENING TO MUSIC ON HIS IPOD, AND READING BOOKS BY PEOPLE LIKE BRENNAN MANNING AND DAVID SEDARIS. HE AND HIS WIFE ARE TIRED OF MEDIOCRITY. THEY WANT TO DO SOMETHING TO HELP A BROKEN SOCIETY—THEY JUST DON'T KNOW HOW. A TWENTY-FIVE-YEAR-OLD SINGLE WOMAN FROM PHOENIX, ARIZONA, LOVES SCRAPBOOKING, SPENDING QUIET NIGHTS AT HOME, AND TALKING ON HER CELL PHONE. HER BEST FRIEND IN NEW YORK CITY THINKS SHE'S CRAZY FOR REMAINING IN PHOENIX. BUT SHE HAS NO PLANS TO MOVE. DESPITE HOW DIFFERENT THEIR LIVES SEEM, ALL OF THESE INDIVIDUALS SHARE ONE THING IN COMMON: THEY ARE EXPERIENCING CULTURE. ALTHOUGH CULTURE CAN BE HARD TO DEFINE, IT IS HAPPENING ALL AROUND US. IN FACT, CULTURE NEVER *STOPS* HAPPENING. AN INDIVIDUAL'S CULTURE DEFINES WHAT LANGUAGE HE SPEAKS, WHAT RELIGION HE FOLLOWS, WHAT MUSIC HE LIKES, AND WHAT KIND OF FOOD HE EATS. BUT IT HARDLY STOPS THERE. CULTURE ALSO INFLUENCES PEOPLE'S PERSONAL BELIEFS, POLITICS, SOCIAL VALUES, ENTERTAINMENT CHOICES, EDUCATION, AND MORE. CULTURE IS THE ENVIRONMENT THAT INFLUENCES YOU, DEFINES YOU, INTERESTS YOU, AND MAKES YOU *YOU*. IF YOU'RE A FOLLOWER OF JESUS, NO DOUBT YOU DESIRE TO HAVE AN IMPACT ON THE WORLD AROUND YOU. YOU PROBABLY ALREADY RALLY AROUND CAUSES THAT MEAN SOMETHING TO YOU, BOTH WITH YOUR FINANCES AND WITH YOUR TIME. IT'S YOUR HEART'S DESIRE TO GET INVOLVED IN MINISTRY, THE POLITICAL PROCESS, AND SOCIAL-SUPPORT PROGRAMS. NOW'S THE TIME TO LEARN TO INTEGRATE YOUR FAITH INTO YOUR CULTURE WITH EASE. WE KNOW IT'S YOUR DESIRE TO BE A BALANCED INDIVIDUAL, AND FRANKLY, WE BELIEVE ALL WORK AND NO PLAY WILL MAKE YOU BORING, TIRED, AND INEFFECTIVE. THAT'S WHY WE'VE INCLUDED THIS CHAPTER ABOUT CULTURE. WE DON'T WANT OUR ADVICE TO DEFINE YOU; WE JUST WANT TO HELP YOU UNDERSTAND THAT CULTURE DOESN'T HAVE TO BE CONFUSING, OVERBEARING, OR INTIMIDATING. WE WANT TO HELP YOU INFLUENCE YOUR CULTURE AND PERHAPS CHALLENGE YOU TO GIVE ANOTHER CULTURE A CHANCE TO TEACH YOU SOMETHING. SO HANG ON TIGHT. YOU'RE ABOUT TO VENTURE INTO AN EXCITING, FUN, AND HOPEFULLY INSPIRING CHAPTER ABOUT CULTURE.

CULTURE

INVEST IN YOUR NEIGHBORHOOD, COMMUNITY, NATION, AND WORLD

WE HAVE A RESPONSIBILITY as people of faith to look for opportunities to serve others. Isn't that what Jesus commanded us to do? Consider Matthew 20:26-28: "But among you it will be different. Whoever wants to be a leader among you must be your servant, and whoever wants to be first among you must become your slave. For even the Son of Man came not to be served but to serve others and to give his life as a ransom for many." If you want to make a difference in this world, be like Christ, and find a cause to be passionate about. When you begin to reach out and meet the needs of others, you will find your own life's needs met too.

In 2003, the world was wowed when Bono used his iconic popularity to heighten awareness of the thousands of people dying each year in Africa from HIV-AIDS. Not only did Bono help awaken Washington, D.C., lawmakers to this modern plague, but he also prompted the church to respond to the crisis. Bono said that it was his faith in God that pushed him to respond to this great need. *Time* magazine even put Bono's mug on its cover and asked the question, "Can Bono save the world?" Sure, it's pretty ridiculous to think that Bono could save the world. But his humanitarian work is a great example of how a person of faith ought to invest in the needs and concerns of culture.

The great thing about investing in culture is that you don't have to be someone like Bono to do it—and you certainly don't have to go to Africa. In most cases, you don't even have to leave your own community.

Twenty-five-year-old Renee Larson makes five hundred dollars a week working as a server at a popular restaurant in Springfield, Missouri. Larson says that for six months she looked for an opportunity to serve in her community to no avail. Her church had community activities, but none of the church volunteer opportunities fit her busy schedule. So she began praying. Eventually, one of her friends who worked at a local nursing home told her that they were looking for a volunteer to help the residents on game night. Larson wasn't necessarily excited about doing this, but because it worked with her schedule, she decided to jump in.

Larson fell in love with the old people—even the grumpy ones. "I never would have imagined enjoying this kind of work. I've actually gotten several of my friends to be involved too. [The nursing home gig] was the first 'need' that worked with my schedule, but little did I know that I needed them, too. They actually helped me!"

When you give your life away to a neighbor, homeless shelter, orphanage, third world country, or nursing home, you will ultimately find your own life fulfilled. Look around you. What are the needs of those on your college campus? in your apartment complex? in your town? in your city? What are the needs of your next-door neighbor? It doesn't matter how big or small the need—it's all about whether or not you're willing to take the time to invest yourself.

Okay, so you might not want to be the next Michael Moore. On top of the fact that he's really unhealthy looking and has poor taste in clothes, much of what he does is counterproductive. However, whether or not you're a fan of Michael Moore or President Bush, the political process *needs* you to be involved.

First of all, it's your right as an American citizen to be involved. You should be taking advantage of that. And second, in order for a democracy to work, the country needs your active participation.

Maybe you're thinking, *Most politicians are liars and cheaters, and I would rather hang out with death-row inmates than spend one ounce of my energy getting a dirty, rotten, power-driven individual elected to public office.* You're not alone in your frustration. But many people who have this opinion haven't checked out the facts and are simply taking the easy way by believing the stereotypes.

It really is important to get educated about the political process. Yeah, social science may not be the most interesting of topics. But let's face it: You probably didn't pay much attention to your civics teacher in high school, so you could use a refresher course on how it all works. Go to www.whitehouse.gov for a quick reminder of how the judicial, executive, and legislative branches work together to give you a say in the direction this country should go. (We'll wait right here while you go get reacquainted with politics. No really—it's quite fine. We like to wait.)

Unless you simply moved on to this paragraph without following the above instructions, you're a political expert now, right? (You're lying, aren't you? You didn't do any refresher course. At least when politicians lie, it takes a scandal to bring out the truth—you've got it written all over your face.) Nonetheless, let's move on.

By far the biggest excuse young adults give for why they refuse to be involved in politics is laziness. Yeah, *laziness!* Most twentys who decide not to vote or not to take a stand for their beliefs just don't *feel* like it. (We won't go into how pathetic this is.)

It's vital that every individual get involved in the political process. So often, it's through politics that social injustices are (or aren't) made right. It is through the political process that important freedoms are made secure. And it's the political process that paves the way for our country to head in new directions.

Maybe politicians aren't the most honest people on the planet, but your involvement can only help the process. Be involved. Make sure your opinion is heard. **AND ALWAYS VOTE!**

BE POLITICAL, OPINIONATED, AND INVOLVED (YOUR COUNTRY NEEDS YOU)

☑ *Vote*

Set your Internet homepage to www.bbcnews.com. It's like reading *The National Enquirer* and watching MSNBC all in one. But if you *really* want to be informed, and you have a budget for such things, subscribe to *The New York Times* or *USA Today*.

Once a week, go to your local Borders or Barnes & Noble and read at least five magazines. And only one of these magazines can be about cars, tattoos, fashion, or video games.

BE INFORMED—
THE COOLEST WAYS TO STAY IN THE KNOW

If you can afford a few magazine subscriptions, make them *Entertainment Weekly, Entrepreneur, Relevant,* and *Shape* or *Men's Fitness.*

Make a point to wake up with Katie and Matt from the *Today Show.* Yes, Katie's a little perky, but you non-morning people can just keep things mellow by turning down the volume.

For everything remotely Christian in the mainstream media, check out www.rockrebel.com. This Web site links to every major story dealing with Christianity in pop culture around the world.

If you're conservative, check out www.drudgereport.com for the latest news and political information with a "red state" slant. And if you're a "blue" supporter, go to www.ofrankenfactor.com.

Lastly, check out www.relevantmagazine.com and www.TwentysOnline.com for Christian information about God and culture.

CULTURE

KNOWING REALLY IS HALF THE BATTLE.

WHEN IT COMES TO RECOGNIZING YOUR PLACE IN CULTURE, A LOT COMES DOWN TO BEING AWARE OF WHAT'S AROUND YOU. IN OTHER WORDS, YOU HAVE TO KNOW YOUR ENVIRONMENT. WHETHER YOU LIVE IN A CITY THAT'S KNOWN FOR ITS CULTURAL HEIGHTS (THINK NEW YORK, CHICAGO, LONDON, OR TOKYO) OR YOU LIVE IN CHEYENNE, WYOMING, WHERE THE CULTURE CONSISTS OF NATIVE AMERICAN RELICS AND COWBOYS RIDING BULLS—THE MORE YOU KNOW ABOUT THE INS AND OUTS OF YOUR COMMUNITY, THE MORE YOU CAN HAVE AN IMPACT. ONCE YOU KNOW, YOU CAN BEGIN TO RELATE. AND WHEN WE RELATE TO THOSE AROUND US, WE'RE SHARING THE LOVE OF CHRIST.

TWENTY THINGS EVERY CULTURE-CONSCIOUS TWENTY SHOULD POSSESS

(It's not that we're materialistic; we simply feel that these things can truly enhance an individual's way of life.)

1 *THE MESSAGE*—Eugene Peterson's paraphrase of the Bible makes it easier to understand.

2 iPOD—How can the ability to carry a bazillion songs around in your pocket *ever* be a bad thing?

3 A GYM MEMBERSHIP—Unless you have a SoloFlex at home, spend forty bucks a month on firming up your buttocks. Come on—twentys want to look sexy too.

4 ONLINE CAPABILITY—Unless you're living in the Dark Ages, you should already have this.

5 A SMOOTHIE KING ADDICTION—Smoothie shops are quickly becoming the new Starbucks. If you think we're kidding, try a Caribbean Way with an extra shot of kiwi—you'll be hooked!

6 AN OPEN MIND—Open up your mind to the thoughts and opinions of others and you will almost always win.

7 A GOOD BOOK—When you read, you get smarter. If you're not an avid reader, pick up the habit. A good book is the perfect conversation starter.

8 A DAILY STRETCH ROUTINE—Flexibility (yes, like a gymnast) is imperative to mobility when you are old. The more flexible you are now, the better you'll feel when you're forty and the more energy you'll have now. Trust us on this one!

9 A JOURNAL—Writing down your thoughts, ideas, and prayers can be very therapeutic.

10 A NICE BLACK OUTFIT—You never know when appearance is going to be everything. Black is thinning, formal, fancy, respectful, and almost always appropriate. Whether it's for a funeral or a job interview, you'll be prepared.

11 A FAVORITE PLACE TO HANG OUT—All of us need a place to go where everyone knows our names. It will impress your date, mom and dad, boss, and even your friends when you walk into your favorite little place and the guy behind the counter calls you by your first name.

12 A LAPTOP COMPUTER—Desktops are out! Most twentys live life on the run—the ability to take your life with you is crucial.

13 A COOL NICKNAME—We're not sure why . . . we just like nicknames.

14 A DVD EDITION OF YOUR FAVORITE TV SHOW—Whether it's *Alias*, *24*, *The Simpsons*, or *Seinfeld* you love, get it on DVD. These collections are great for big parties, small get-togethers, and just when you want to be entertained!

15 A TRAVEL BUDGET—Unlike your parents, you don't mind seeing the rest of the world *before* you see the Grand Canyon and Old Faithful. Save up and go somewhere!

16 A SUBSCRIPTION TO *ENTERTAINMENT WEEKLY*—It's hard work keeping up with pop culture. *EW* is a relatively inexpensive way to at least attempt to.

17 A LOVE FOR THAI OR INDIAN FOOD—Ethnic food will always be in. Expand your food horizons beyond hamburgers.

18 A PASSPORT—When travel calls, a passport ensures there's no chance that you'll be left behind!

19 AN EXPENSIVE PAIR OF SHOES—Your feet are important. Pamper and protect them with a good pair of shoes. You'll thank us when you're sixty!

20 A DIGITAL CAMERA—You don't want to forget all of the cool things you've done over the years!

MY FIVE FAVORITE MOVIES
(WRITTEN BY MARTIN LUTHER'S PRETEND GHOST)

Most of you naïve nincompoops don't have any idea who I am, do you? No, I'm not the guy who gave the "I Have a Dream" speech. Some days I wish I had been him. *He* got a holiday named after him. *He* gets great publicity. All I get is a little name recognition from silly seminary students who think *C. S. Lewis* was a scholar. Fiddlesticks! I would rather have had the holiday.

Those of you who do have an inkling of who I am are asking yourselves, *Isn't he dead?* Goodness, yes—of course I'm dead. I've been dead for more than 450 years. But from time to time people ask me to make commentary on popular culture. And why shouldn't they? My famous ninety-five reasons for why the Catholic church in my day stunk changed the course of religious history. You wouldn't be enjoying your rock and roll in church on Sunday mornings without me. Rick Warren would be *nothing* without me. He owes me—the concepts behind *The Purpose Driven Life* were *my* idea.

But alas, I digress. I was asked to write a little feature for this book on my favorite life-changing movies. You might be thinking, *How do you get to see movies?* Well, just because we saints walk through pearly gates every morning doesn't mean we don't keep up with pop culture. I'm a phat dude. And surprisingly, God is actually quite the movie buff. Don't tell anyone, but he's a big sci-fi fan. Of course, St. Augustine insists we buy the edited versions of all the movies—he's such a brownnoser. Anyway, enough of my bickering. Here's my list of the top five:

DEAD MAN WALKING—Sean Penn and Susan Sarandon may be liberal, good-for-nothing posers, but they sure can act. No doubt about that.

NAPOLEON DYNAMITE—John Calvin and I laughed our heads off over this one. Of course, Calvin went on and on about how God was the one who chose how the movie ended. But I told him he was going too far. God would never have chosen an ending that included break dancing.

BEN-HUR—The heavens came down and glory filled our souls when this epic won Best Picture in 1959. On a side note and just between you and me, Mother Teresa has always had a thing for Charlton Heston.

LES MISERABLES—Why did it take Hollywood so long to turn this Hugo novel into a movie? Jean Valjean is certainly one of the most compelling characters in all of literature. And this movie makes the French leaders look totally ridiculous—you Americans have got to love that.

THE LORD OF THE RINGS TRILOGY—Tolkien and I play poker together. *He* made me include this one.

CELEBRATE NEW YEAR'S EVE
· · · · · · · · · · · · · · · ·AND THE OTHER BIG HOLIDAYS?

Ever since time began, or at least as long as Dick Clark has been around, New Year's Eve has been the biggest party night of the year. And there are plenty of other partying opportunities throughout the year too—St. Patrick's Day, Cinco de Mayo, the Fourth of July, Halloween, and of course, Christmas!

Here's a helpful guide to making the most of your next big party opportunity:

THE GET-OUT-OF-THE-HOUSE OPTION

There are many ways to find great ideas for your holiday out on the town. Check the local paper for information about fireworks displays, concerts, special hotel deals, and more. Make sure you do your research! Many holiday events are pricey and may not offer nonalcoholic settings.

If the regular nightlife is not your style, find out if any local churches are hosting events with a Christian flair. Although many church-affiliated parties are not quite as elaborate as the scene around town, many churches' events, concerts, and theme parties are actually a great alternative to the party scene.

Another option is to party hop. Hopping from party to party is a great way to meet new, interesting people. And that way you don't have to commit to spending your whole evening in one spot.

ADVICE FOR GOING OUT

1 Know the dress code. It's never cool to show up under- or overdressed for an engagement.

2 Take some cash with you. Many private events do not have credit card access. And in today's cashless society, that could be disastrous and embarrassing for you and your date.

3 If you live in a large city, you might want to consider public transportation. It's usually cheaper and safer than driving in on your own.

4 If you're going to a friend or colleague's party, you might want to take a small gift for the host. It certainly doesn't have to be extravagant, but it's always a nice gesture of appreciation.

5 Plan ahead. If you're planning to go out with friends, why not get together with them a few days beforehand to schedule your evening and ensure that everyone has a say in the plans?

6 Unless you're planning to eat at McDonald's or Subway, call the restaurant at least two weeks in advance to see if it's accepting holiday reservations.

THE BRING-THE-PARTY-TO-YOU OPTION

While going out is fun and adventurous, it might be even better to throw a bash of your own. Although it may seem like a huge undertaking, a little ahead-of-time planning can make it a whole lot simpler.

A VERY FEW GOOD MEN

DID YOU KNOW?

According to the 2000 census, nearly 2 percent more women than men live in the United States.

ADVICE ON THROWING THE

① DEFINE YOUR PARTY. Will you have a theme? How many people do you want to invite? What will the evening entail? Don't sweat this—just take a few moments to think about your party options and plan accordingly.

② INVITE YOUR FRIENDS. Although most party professionals recommend sending out invitations, it's a good idea to telephone your peeps too. Give them the heads up over the phone and then follow it up with an invite, e-vite (www.evite.com), or e-mail. Remember, your friends may have lots of options, and you want to make sure they are well aware of *your* party.

③ CHOOSE YOUR MUNCHIES. Don't go overboard on food. Finger food, crackers and cheese, veggie trays, chips and salsa, and a couple of dessert options are more than enough. It's better to keep the menu small with big quantities than to try to impress your guests with a luxurious spread of a million choices. If you're up for a few "special" food items, why not go to www.allrecipes.com and make something new? Also, you might consider asking a few of your friends to help you out by bringing something with them when they come.

④ DECORATE! Although this is certainly not the most important aspect of your party, it is a nice extravagance that adds a lot. Check out www.shindigz.com or www.partypro.com for some inexpensive ideas.

⑤ TURN UP THE MUSIC! An absolute must for any successful party is the right music—and lots of it. Do whatever you have to do to get a good mix of songs that everyone will enjoy. If you opt for a theme party, it might be fun to have some background music that matches the theme. If you're clueless about what music to buy, check out www.itunes.com or www.walmart.com. Both of these Web sites provide thirty-second samples of all their songs. And Wal-Mart sells the G-rated versions of all the popular songs—something that might come in handy!

⑥ HAVE FUN! No matter what, make sure you and your guests have a blast. Don't stress about what goes wrong or who doesn't show up. The name of the game is *fun*.

CULTURE QUOTES " "

Napoleon Dynamite: (in reference to the dance) "Who are you gonna ask?" Pedro: "That girl over there." Napoleon Dynamite: "Summer Wheatley? How the heck are you gonna do that?" Pedro: "Build her a cake or something."

—(*Source:* Napoleon Dynamite, *2004*)

WHEN YOUR BEST FRIEND COMES OUT OF THE CLOSET...

BY SAMANTHA STINE*

My friend Johnny has one of the best singing voices I have ever heard. I met him the year I joined the teen choir at the very traditional church my grandparents attend. We became instant friends because of our mutual love of dc talk, Madonna, and the TV show *My So-Called Life.* When we graduated from high school, Johnny gave me a Bible and wrote these words in it: "Stay in the Word, girl. I love you, Johnny."

I must admit—I had a crush on Johnny. All the girls did. He was good-looking, a great dresser, sensitive, a dreamer, easy to talk to, a go-getter . . . and gay. Yes, gay. Of course, I didn't know that he was gay until my junior year of college. And I'm glad I didn't. Because if I had known Johnny was gay, I'm not sure we would have been friends. Sad, huh?

I'll never forget the day Johnny told me. We were home for Christmas break from college—I went to the state school in my town and Johnny was studying engineering at a well-known, Christian university. We were catching up over coffee when he looked at me and said, "I have something very important I need to share with you." Instantly, I feared the worst—perhaps he was dying, engaged to be married, or moving away to Africa to become a missionary. "I'm gay," he said as tears began to stream down his cute, shy face.

"What!?!" I exclaimed. "You're gay? But you're a Christian. Christians can't be gay."

"Please don't hate me, Samantha. You're the first person I have had the guts to tell this to," he said, looking at me intently.

I was speechless at first. I didn't know what to say. At that moment I honestly think I hated him for telling me. He knew how I felt about homosexuality. He knew what the Bible says about it. What was I supposed to say to him?

After what seemed to be forever, I finally mustered up enough energy to say, "Johnny, I love you. I will always love you. You have to give me some time to deal with this, but know that I am here for you."

When I got home, I went to my bedroom and sobbed. A million ideas began rolling through my head. Perhaps I could pray his gayness away. That didn't work. Perhaps he could go to counseling. Therapy didn't make him straight. Perhaps it was simply a stage. Needless to say, it wasn't just a stage. I had to find a way to cope with my best friend in the world being gay. And that's *not* something they teach in Sunday school.

While many disowned him after they heard the news, I decided I was going to remain his friend. Johnny knows that I don't agree with him, but I choose to love him despite my feelings. We respect each other's views. He knows that I think his lifestyle is wrong, but I feel that I am more of a help being involved in his life than not.

Sure, sometimes I still pray that one day he'll come to me and tell me he is not gay. But I don't hold my breath, and my friendship with him is not contingent on that happening. •

* Names have been changed.

THIRTEEN ALBUMS
THE SOUND TRACKS OF OUR LIVES

1. *Joshua Tree* by **U2**—No, this is not a praise and worship album. But it's soooo good!

2. *Dangerous* by **Michael Jackson**—Okay, so we're not sure how cool Michael is today, but songs like "Black and White" and "Remember the Time" sure make us want to revel in what once was.

3. *A Rush of Blood to the Head* by **Coldplay**—We're not sure this British band can do anything musically wrong.

4. *Down with the King* by **Run-DMC**—For when you just want to relive high school.

5. *Jagged Little Pill* by **Alanis Morissette**—Yes, we know she drops a bad word in one or two of the songs, but the songwriting on Alanis's first take is eye-opening.

6. *Automatic for the People* by **R.E.M.**—"Everybody Hurts" and everybody listened.

7. *She's So Unusual* by **Cyndi Lauper**—"Girls Just Want to Have Fun" is still a staple at weddings, bachelorette parties, and sleepovers.

8. *The Beautiful Letdown* by **Switchfoot**—I "Dare You to Move" because you were "Meant to Live" for so much more. This album is like having your own little therapy session and pep rally all in one.

9. *No More Drama* by **Mary J. Blige**—If you've never been out on the dance floor when Ms. Blige's "Family Affair" is booming through the loud speakers, you've never danced.

10. *So* by **Peter Gabriel**—An eighties class act whose music still matters today.

11. *Survivor* by **Destiny's Child**—As they say in the song: "They ain't gonna compromise their Christianity."

12. *The Miseducation of Lauryn Hill* by **Lauryn Hill**—Hip-hop never said so much and sounded so good.

13. *Norah Jones* by **Norah Jones**—She made listening to our parents' music bearable.

YOU ARE THE HANDS, FEET, AND MOUTH OF JESUS ●●●

JESUS SAYS IN MATTHEW 5:14 that you are like a city on a hill. As a twenty, you have a unique opportunity to live out those words of Christ. Already, the nation is looking to you to see what America's future holds. What are you showing them? Well, you spend a lot of money—on your Visa. You like to travel—spring break was big for you. You grew up on MTV. How about the fact that you love Jesus? Here are some tangible ways you can be the hands, feet, and mouth of Jesus:

VOLUNTEER

Jesus had a heart for those in need, and so should you. If you don't know where to start, call up your church or your local Chamber of Commerce. Both should be able to provide you with names of community organizations that need help. Service opportunities are broad, and chances are you will find something that suits your gifts and abilities.

PRAY

Jesus prayed constantly, both with others and by himself. Never doubt that the Father hears the words you lift up in prayer. Pray throughout your day—it will change your life.

TALK THE TALK

Though it can be easy to talk like the world—a cuss word here, a bit of gossip there—speaking like that is not allowing Jesus to work through you. Scripture says, "Don't use foul or abusive language. Let everything you say be good and helpful, so that your words will be an encouragement to those who hear them" (Ephesians 4:29).

GO

Whether you go to your neighbor's and help her take out her garbage or go to Africa and love on little children—Jesus commands us to go out and be salt and light to the world (Matthew 5:13-16). For some people that means Asia, but for some it might mean Aunt Susan's. It doesn't matter, as long as you are being obedient to God's call on your life.

YOU MIGHT BE STEREOTYPICALLY "POSTMODERN" IF . . .

... You've ever considered U2's music to be worship.

... You think Eugene Peterson wrote the Bible.

... You consider the Passion conferences to be your Woodstock.

... You thought the book *Walk On* was better than C. S. Lewis's *Mere Christianity.*

... You have your own blog where you do your complaining.

... You have verbally slandered WWJD bracelets.

... You use the word *relevant* to describe how everything should be.

... You feel that you can worship better with candles and chants than peppy hymns and fluorescents.

... You ever refer to yourself as a "roaring lamb."

... You roll your eyes when *tobyMac* and *hip-hop* are used in the same sentence.

" CULTURE QUOTES

"Until the philosophy which holds one race superior and another inferior is finally and permanently discredited and abandoned, everywhere is war and until there are no longer first-class and second-class citizens of any nation, until the color of a man's skin is of no more significance than the color of his eyes. And until the basic human rights are equally guaranteed to all without regard to race, there is war. And until that day, the dream of lasting peace, world citizenship, rule of international morality, will remain but a fleeting illusion to be pursued, but never attained. . . . Now everywhere is war."

—Bob Marley

BE THE PENCIL

Mother Teresa once said, "I am just a little pencil in the hand of a loving God, writing a love letter to the world." Remember that you might be the only love letter some people receive. Allow God to use you to bless and love others.

GIVE YOUR LIFE AWAY

Above all, remember that your life is not yours anyway. You don't take anything on this earth with you when you die. Keep that eternal perspective, with your eyes focused on things above. By being unselfish, you will experience Christ through your investment into the lives of other people. Jesus asked us to be salt and light. It wasn't a simple request like, "Hey, while you're serving me, can you serve others too?" It was a bold command to serve God by serving others. • • • • • • • •

THREE EXPERIENCES YOU SHOULD DEFINITELY HAVE BEFORE YOU DIE
• •

A FOREIGN MISSIONS TRIP. Whether it's with a church group helping a missionary family or an organization inviting anyone and everyone to Peru for two weeks to work with the poor, find a cause you believe in and go! If you are at a loss for ideas, speak with your church's missions pastor about possibilities. Tell him you have a heart to go overseas and help out. Check out the travel section at TwentysOnline.com for upcoming trips specifically designed for people in their twentys.

A CRUISE. The service on most cruise ships is impeccable. Everyone should get to stay up until two o'clock in the morning devouring everything in sight at the all-you-can-eat chocolate buffet or spend their days exploring tropical islands on a relaxing cruise getaway.

A ROAD TRIP. It doesn't matter where you road trip *to*—the experience itself is exhilarating. Gas up the car, bring a friend along for the journey, listen to music louder than you should, sing along *way* louder than you should, and stop when you get tired.

If you have the time and the cash, we recommend taking a cruise or a road trip or going on a foreign missions trip, but more important than traveling the world is taking the time to invest in yourself. You might not be able to afford a trip halfway around the world, but you can take a day off and have a picnic in your favorite park or hike through the nearest national forest. You work hard, and everyone needs to get away from everyday life sometimes.

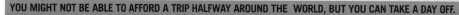

YOU MIGHT NOT BE ABLE TO AFFORD A TRIP HALFWAY AROUND THE WORLD, BUT YOU CAN TAKE A DAY OFF.

7 THINGS YOU SHOULD ALWAYS FIND WHEN VISITING A NEW CITY

THE AMERICAN EMBASSY—If you're in a foreign city, you should always know where the American embassy is located. You never know when you'll need to head for some familiar territory.

THE DOWNTOWN DISTRICT—From Madison, Wisconsin, to Naples, Florida, to Chicago and Houston, many cities are redesigning their downtowns as places to get down in the town. Ask your hotel's concierge where you should go, or look up the best spots online.

MUSEUMS—Whether you're into art, history, or science, go to the museums! They offer a unique chance to experience a city's history, culture, and character.

WHERE THE CELEBRITIES HANG OUT—Not every city has such a place, but many do. Find out where all the bigwigs eat lunch, and then go there and see who you run into. If you do spot someone, you'll be talking about it for years!

TOURIST TRAPS—Always allow yourself one touristy indulgence. Whether it's the Empire State Building in New York or Buckingham Palace in London, sometimes the tourist traps are fun and exciting. Even South of the Border on the North/South Carolina border can be a fun little place to stop!

THE BAD SIDE OF TOWN—Find out where it is and then avoid it unless you're with someone who knows her way around.

WHERE THE LOCALS HANG OUT—After you've visited where the celebrities and tourists hang out, find out where those who know the city best like to commune. It will probably end up being your favorite place to chill.

BASIC ADVICE FOR AMERICANS TRAVELING TO A THIRD-WORLD COUNTRY ⟫⟫⟫⟫⟫⟫⟫⟫⟫⟫⟫

DON'T DRINK THE WATER OR ANYTHING WASHED IN OR MADE OF IT (ESPECIALLY ICE).

DON'T REACT TO EVERYTHING THAT IS PLACED IN FRONT OF YOU WITH, "THAT'S NOT HOW IT LOOKS/TASTES/SMELLS IN THE UNITED STATES!"

EMBRACE THE FACT THAT YOU WILL EXPERIENCE CULTURE SHOCK IN SOME WAY, SHAPE, OR FORM NO MATTER HOW OPEN-MINDED YOU ARE. TRY TO AVOID MAKING YOURSELF MORE COMFORTABLE BY MAKING JOKES ABOUT THE THINGS THAT ARE UNFAMILIAR.

DON'T BE "THAT" AMERICAN . . . WAXING POETIC ABOUT THOSE THINGS IN THE UNITED STATES THAT MAKE US BETTER THAN ALL OTHER COUNTRIES. INSTEAD, COME HOME MORE THANKFUL THAT YOU LIVE WHERE YOU DO.

DON'T WEAR OPEN-TOED ANYTHING. NEVER. NOT EVEN OPEN FOR DISCUSSION.

DON'T FORGET TO TAKE ASPIRIN AND ANTIBIOTICS ALONG WITH YOU.

DON'T MESS AROUND WITH BEING CHEAP WITH YOUR SHOTS. GET 'EM ALL. TAKE THE MALARIA PILLS EVEN IF THE THOUGHT OF SWALLOWING SOMETHING ALIVE FREAKS YOU OUT.

DON'T FORGET TO BREATHE DEEPLY AND REMEMBER THE SMELLS AND SOUNDS OF PLACES YOU MAY NEVER WALK AGAIN. ⟫⟫⟫

SETTLING IN: AN IN-DEPTH LOOK AT
MOVING FAR AWAY

CROSS-COUNTRY MOVES ARE BECOMING more and more common among twentys. You land the dream job and set your face toward the promised land. A mad flurry of activity surrounds your final days in the familiar world you're leaving behind. Last-minute packing woes, good-bye parties every night for a week, a cleaning frenzy to avoid penalties from the place you're vacating . . . chaos on every side. But fun chaos because you know everyone and everything around here. You load up the moving truck or car, get up at the crack of dawn, and set out for the greener pastures you've always dreamed of.

Many hours later, you finally arrive at your destination. You make your grand entrance tired and stinky from too much time in the car. With lease papers signed and the truck unloaded, you finally get a chance to sit and rest. Ah . . . relief!

Then something crazy happens. The boxes you packed just last week start multiplying right before your eyes. They taunt you with an overwhelming sense of "I'll-never-find-a-place-for-all-this." The bare walls echo lonely, haunting refrains that cut to the bone. Suddenly the cold, hard floor you're sitting on sends a chill right through you. You're so alone. Every friend you have is hundreds of miles away. The lump in your throat grows. Eyes blink rapidly. How will this place ever feel like home? What have you done?

When you find yourself far away from everything and everyone familiar, don't freak out. Resist the urge to pack those boxes right back up and head home to your old life. There are ways you can help smooth out the transition.

PLUG IN IMMEDIATELY

The best thing you can do for yourself is meet as many new people as possible in the first day or two. Try a church service or small group. Meet your neighbors. If you live in an apartment or dorm, make friends with the staff. The sooner you can connect with others, the sooner you will establish a home here.

LEAN ON YOUR OLD FRIENDS

Just because they're forever away does not mean you can't call or e-mail, especially during those first few weeks in new surroundings. Tell them all your adventures and settling-in tales. It'll be easier to hang in there and do your best if someone knows where you are and what you're going through, even if they're in another state.

MAKE THE SPACE "YOU"

Putting up familiar pictures or drinking coffee out of your favorite mug can go a long way toward making things more comfortable. Don't leave those fun, personal touches until last in the unpacking process. Do them first, and then finish the boring stuff like clothes and shoes later.

GET OUT

Out of necessity, you'll find the nearest grocery store and Target within the first day or so. But don't settle with that. See what else there is. Go out and enjoy an afternoon of exploration around town. Check out the local stores, neighborhoods, and parks. Locate the movie theater, Starbucks, and the nearest hospital. Whatever you do, don't just sit at home wishing you were somewhere else.

CULTURE QUOTES 66 99

> **"The nice part of living in a small town is that when I don't know what I'm doing, someone else does."**
>
> —Source Unknown

> **"Memories are the key not to the past, but to the future."**
>
> ——Corrie ten Boom

GIVE IT A CHANCE

Don't expect things to be perfect and easy right away. And don't try to force friendships with strangers who aren't really interested. Just be patient. Recognize that you're in a time of flux and that it won't always be this way. Spend those lonely hours working on your character, spending time with God, reading, or working out. Before you know it, you'll find yourself somehow immersed in a new version of familiar. What was uncomfortable and forced at first will be peaceful and natural. And the walls will echo happy refrains instead of haunting ones! • • • • • • • •

TEN RULES FOR A SMOOTH TRANSITION
When Moving Someplace outside the United States

① Don't complain about your new environment. You chose to move, and you knew it was going to be different.

② Don't let others get on your nerves. When you move to a new place, expect people to be different, just like the climate, the clothes, the food, etc. You have come a long way to learn as much as you can. Enjoy the experience.

③ Make a habit of *listening* and *observing*, rather than merely *hearing* and *seeing*.

④ Avoid making promises that you cannot carry through for your new local friends. Most people have long memories.

⑤ Know where your passport is at all times. A person without a passport is a person without a country.

⑥ You shall remember that you are a guest in every land. One who treats a host with respect will be treated as an honored guest.

⑦ Spend time reflecting on each day in order to deepen your understanding of your experiences.

⑧ Educate yourself about the country you're visiting. The Internet offers a great deal of information. For more in-depth information, visit your local bookstore or library.

⑨ When you travel, do it with a spirit of humility and with a genuine desire to meet and talk to local people. In other words, don't be a complete donkey-butt.

⑩ Realize that other people may have thought patterns and concepts of time that are very different from yours—not inferior, just different.

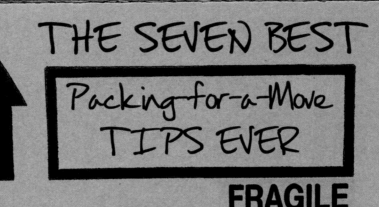

THE SEVEN BEST
Packing-for-a-Move TIPS EVER

FRAGILE

1. Pack a suitcase with a week's worth of clothes and toiletries. Also include at least two rolls of toilet paper, a large trash bag, a shower curtain, and a set of sheets and towels. Put this in the truck last or carry it with you.

2. Lay clothes flat and then roll them up tightly. You'll fit way more into a small space that way. Use bulky sweaters, blankets, and jackets as insulation in boxes of your fragile belongings.

3. Be overly anal about breakables. Wrap them carefully and mark the boxes "fragile" in large letters.

4. Tape the remote control to the TV, and do the same with the cords to all of your appliances. Otherwise, there's a good chance you'll never see them again.

5. Pack books in small boxes or spread them out among other belongings. Big boxes of books are miserably heavy and hard to move.

6. Be creative with how you pack. Fill every hollow space in washers and dryers, pitchers, shoes, baskets, etc.

7. Load furniture and large boxes first, then fill in with smaller boxes, fragiles, plants, and loose items.

CHECKLIST FOR EASY MOVING

- ☑ Spend time now with special friends and family members. Plan out your moving commitments ahead of time so you'll have plenty of time with loved ones before moving day arrives.

- ☑ Plan ahead for packing. Start collecting boxes from grocery stores or warehouse discount chains (like Sam's or Costco).

- ☑ Purge closets, drawers, and shelves of everything you don't truly need. Give away anything you haven't seen . . . and haven't missed . . . in the last three years.

- ☑ Clearly label every box with its general contents and what room or area it belongs to.

- ☑ Compare prices among truck-rental agencies or moving companies.

- ☑ If you're moving for a new job, ask your employer about their relocation policy.

- ☑ Research the reputation of different areas in the new city and then check apartment or real estate guides and local classifieds for potential places to live.

- ☑ Contact churches, community groups, or school organizations to ask if they know of anyone looking for a roommate.

- ☑ Make a list of people and companies to notify of your new address and check them off as you call them.

- ☑ Complete a "Change of Address" form at the Post Office.

- ☑ Research churches ahead of time so you have one to try out in your new city the very first week.

- ☑ Line up helpers. Enlist buddies to help load and unload the moving truck.

- ☑ Get everything packed in time to clean your old place before you leave.

- ☑ Pay deposits and setup fees for utilities in the new place ahead of time so there's no waiting for service once you arrive.

- ☑ Schedule a few extra days for unpacking and errands such as grocery shopping, driver's license change, and voter registration before you start work or school.

> ❝❞ **CULTURE QUOTES**
>
> **"Greater love hath no man than this, that a man lay down his life for his friends."**
>
> **–Jesus (John 15:13, KJV)**

SEVEN WAYS TO GET TO KNOW YOUR NEIGHBORS

❶ Old-Fashioned Style—Make an apple pie and take it to them. (If you don't know how to make a pie, take them Oreos—everybody likes Oreos.)

❷ Fun Style—Have poker night at your place and invite your neighbors to play. (Or if you're against playing cards, play Yahtzee. If you're against playing with dice—play Uno. Doh!)

❸ Hard-Work Style—If you see new people moving in next door, volunteer to help—people always need help moving in. (Yes, we know you hate moving boxes, but do it anyway.)

❹ Country Style—Have a yard sale. Your neighbors will come in droves.

❺ Entertainment Style—Invite all your neighbors over for chips, salsa, and whatever TV show you're into.

❻ Pet Style—Get a dog. Pets are great tools for meeting the canine-loving people in your apartment complex or community.

❼ Cheap Style—Borrow something from them. This is a foolproof way of getting to know your neighbors. (Ask them for sugar, an egg, a lawn mower. Neighbors usually have everything!)

BETTER SAFE THAN STUPID

A little bit of common sense and purposeful prevention can go a long way when it comes to living in security. You're a grown-up now, so realize no one's going to take care of you except you. Don't be a paranoid freak or anything, but don't throw all caution to the wind, either.

Pay attention to your surroundings.

Walk or jog only in well-lit, well-populated areas.

If you're in a shady situation, try to appear confident and never nervous.

Shout "Fire!" rather than "Help!" More people will pay attention to you that way.

Never approach a stranger's vehicle for any reason.

Know who's around when you cash out at an ATM.

Keep purses or messenger bags close, clasp facing against your body.

Don't keep your wallet, credit cards, phone, and cash all in the same bag or pocket.

Know your neighbors. You may need them some day.

Keep a small fire extinguisher in the kitchen.

Keep doors and windows locked.

Adhere to your vehicle's recommended maintenance schedule.

Just being aware of risks and circumstances can go a long way. Do that and follow the dozen tips above, and you'll live happily ever after. (Hopefully.) • • • • • • • • • • • • • •

FIVE CAUSES TO GET BEHIND

\\

Looking for a trustworthy charity that you can feel good about supporting? Look no further. Here's a list of the Twentys organization's top five choices! **American Heart Association**—The AHA is a wonderful cause to do volunteer work for and a great not-for-profit organization to get behind financially. Either way, you will be helping change lives for the better. Go to **www.americanheart.org** for more information. **Compassion International**—As one of the leading child-relief organizations in the country, Compassion International fights poverty all over the world. For thirty-two dollars a month, you can adopt a child from one of four continents. Go to **www.compassion.com** for more information. **The Persecuted Church**—Millions of Christians all over the world are being persecuted by governments, militants, and religious leaders. You can help! Go to **www.persecutedchurch.org** for information on how you can help people around the world worship Jesus freely. **African Leadership**—Thousands of people die daily in Africa because of the AIDS virus. Even scarier is the truth that many of these people die without knowing the Good News of Jesus Christ. African Leadership is a nonprofit educational and developmental organization that seeks to train local African pastors and fund health and education development in communities throughout the continent. To learn more, go to **www.africanleadership.org**.

The Lance Armstrong Foundation—As a cancer survivor, Lance Armstrong's goal is to make the best cancer treatment available to everyone. His foundation seeks to educate, advocate, and support research. To learn more about this important cause, go to **www.laf.org.**

CULTURE QUOTES 66 99

"Education is the most powerful weapon which you can use to change the world."

—Nelson Mandela

A LIST OF SOME MAJOR EVENTS IN CHRISTIAN HISTORY

2000 B.C. Abraham, the founder of Judaism is alive.

4 B.C. The year most scholars believe Christ was born

A.D. 33 The estimated year of Christ's death and resurrection

48 The estimated year that Paul set out on his first missionary experience

338 The Vulgate was established as the first written form of Scripture

387 Augustine of Hippo wrote his autobiography, *Confessions*

1452 The Gutenberg Bible became the first Bible produced on a printing press

1494 The first Roman Catholic mass in the Americas was celebrated on Isabella Island, Haiti

1517 Martin Luther posted his famous Ninety-Five Theses, causing a great controversy within the Roman Catholic Church

1534 Henry VIII declared himself head of the Anglican Church

1564 John Calvin preached his last sermon three months before his death

1611 The King James Version of the Bible was printed

1621 Pilgrims left the *Mayflower* and gathered onshore at Plymouth, Massachusetts, for their first religious service in America

1730 The First Great Awakening began in England and the American colonies

1742 Handel's famous oratorio *Messiah* premiered

1790 The Second Great Awakening began in England and the United States

1791 John Wesley, founder of Methodism, died in London

1816 The American Bible Society organized in New York to distribute the Bible throughout the world

TEN DEFINING MOMENTS & PEOPLE WE WILL NEVER FORGET

① BILL CLINTON AND MONICA LEWINSKI
What really is the definition of *is?*

② BEAVIS AND BUTT-HEAD AND *THE SIMPSONS*
The Flintstones just don't do it for us anymore.
"Yabba dabba"—I mean, "Don't have a cow, dude!"

③ BRITNEY SPEARS
We wanted you to hit us, baby, one more time, drive us "Crazy," make us "Toxic," and then, oops, do it again!

④ THE OKLAHOMA CITY BOMBING
Somehow we never thought terrorism would ever hit this close to home. This proved us wrong.

⑤ OLYMPIC GYMNAST KERRI STRUG
That little girl inspired all of us to break one of our ankles and then attempt a perfect dismount!

⑥ O. J. SIMPSON
The murder, the car chase, the trial, the verdict.

1837 Famed evangelist Dwight L. Moody was born in Massachusetts

1852 Abolitionist Harriet Beecher Stowe, daughter of famous Congregational minister Lyman Beecher, published *Uncle Tom's Cabin*

1854 Missionary Hudson Taylor landed in Shanghai, China

1864 The motto "In God We Trust," conceived during the Civil War, first appeared on American coinage

1921 Pittsburgh radio station KDKA broadcasted the first religious program over the airwaves

1937 Billy Graham preached for the first time when his teacher John Minder unexpectedly assigned him the Easter evening sermon

1949 Billy Graham skyrocketed to national prominence with an evangelistic crusade in Los Angeles

1956 Missionaries Jim Elliot, Nate Saint, Roger Youderin, Ed McCully, and Peter Fleming were killed by Ecuadorian Indians they sought to evangelize

1965 Baptist minister Martin Luther King Jr. led more than three thousand civil rights demonstrators on a march from Selma, Alabama, to Montgomery

1968 Martin Luther King Jr. was assassinated

1971 The musical *Godspel!*, based on Matthew's Gospel, opened at the Cherry Lane Theater in New York

1971 Kenneth Taylor published *The Living Bible*

1971 The United States Supreme Court legalized abortion in its *Roe v. Wade* decision

1996 Tim LaHaye and Jerry B. Jenkins published *Left Behind*, a mega-best-selling book about the end times

1997 Mother Teresa died in Calcutta, India

2002 Rick Warren published *The Purpose Driven Life*, which sold more than 20 million copies

2004 Mel Gibson made entertainment history with his powerful movie blockbuster *The Passion of the Christ*

---

❼ JANET JACKSON'S SUPER BOWL WARDROBE MALFUNCTION
The generation that thought it could not be shocked was shocked. Really shocked.

❽ THE 2000 ELECTION CONTROVERSY
Some of us may never vote again.

❾ COLUMBINE
The anger of two young men changed our education system forever.

❿ SEPTEMBER 11, 2001—*We will never forget.*

" CULTURE QUOTES

"At home, the job of a president is to help cultures change. The culture needs to be changed. I call it, so people can understand what I'm talking about, changing the culture from one that says, 'If it feels good, do it, and if you've got a problem, blame somebody else,' to a culture in which each of us understands we're responsible for the decisions we make in life. I call it the responsibility era."

—President George W. Bush
(quoted by Christianity Today at
http://www.christianitytoday.com/ct/2004/121/51.0.html.)

about the authors

DAVID EDWARDS is a dynamic author, speaker, and man on a mission. He is known for masterfully applying biblical truths with humor in an honest and understandable form. A gifted communicator, David travels the country full time and has spoken to literally hundreds of thousands of young adults. He holds extensive singles ministry experience, having been a regularly featured speaker for weekly citywide Bible studies in nine states. He has authored five books, including *The God of Yes: Living the Life You Were Promised* (Howard Publishing Company, 2003) and *The Challenge* (LifeWay Publishing, 2000) and has recently released a six-book series called Questions for Life (Cook Communications, October 2004). Unexpected treasures like the CD set *God in a Box* and the evangelistic tract *How to Make Life All Good* sneak under the radar to bring audiences closer to Jesus Christ—one step at a time.

MARGARET FEINBERG is a speaker, author, and freelance writer known for her unique combination of honesty and humor in identifying with audiences. Her book *Twentysomething: Surviving & Thriving in the Real World* (W Publishing, 2004) takes an up close look at the biggest issues facing today's twentys. Her research is based on more than one hundred interviews with pastors, counselors, and researchers, as well as twentys from across the country. Her recent books include *Simple Acts of Faith: Heartwarming Stories of One Life Touching Another* (a Gold Medallion nominee), *Simple Acts of Friendship: Heartwarming Stories of One Friend Blessing Another* (both from Harvest House), and *God Whispers: Learning to Hear His Voice* (Relevant Books). Additionally, she has coauthored or contributed to another five books and written more than seven hundred articles for publications including *CBA Marketplace*, *Christianity Today*, *Charisma*, *New Man*, *Ministries Today*, *BookPage*, and *Christian Retailing*. She lives in Juneau, Alaska, with her 6'8" Norwegian husband.

JANELLA GRIGGS is a former missionary to Central America, writer, and vice president of Twentys, an organization dedicated to helping young adults navigate the spiritual, emotional, mental, physical, and financial changes that normally occur between the ages of twenty and twenty-nine. She is known far and wide for her off-the-cuff humor and unmistakable Southern charm. Janella has written the 2004 International Mission Study (Mexico Times, Woman's Missionary Union, SBC, 2004) and numerous articles, teaching guides, brochures, and strategic planning guides for national and international ministries. She is an established expert in branding, integrated marketing, and managing stakeholder relationships for maximum return. With an all-out passion for Jesus, love for missions, and zeal for reaching others, she spurs audiences toward an authentic, meaningful relationship with the Savior.

MATTHEW PAUL TURNER is a speaker, writer, and visionary who steps outside the expected and into the sublime. He is the former editor of *CCM* magazine, the nation's leading Christian entertainment publication, and former music and entertainment editor of Crosswalk.com, the world's largest Christian Web site. Author of *The Christian Culture Survival Guide: The Misadventures of an Outsider on the Inside* (Relevant Books, 2004) and dozens of published articles for national magazines and Web sites, he is known for shockingly honest portraits of culture, uncompromising passion, and sidesplitting humor. He was a concert booker for the well-known coffeehouse Jammin' Java and is also the founder of God Culture Ministries. His background as a disengaged "church kid" and his subsequent discovery of true grace lend credibility to a generation of alienated twentys who long for restoration.